MESOZOIC ERA

Cretaceous Period:
144–65 millions of years ago

CENOZOIC ERA

Tertiary Period:
65–2 millions
of years ago

Quaternary Period:
65–2 millions
of years ago

THE
ORNITHOPODS

THE AGE OF THE DINOSAURS

THE
ORNITHOPODS

VOLUME 7

GROLIER
EDUCATIONAL

CONTENTS

→ Introduction to the ornithopods

Today's grasslands and forests support many kinds of plant-eating mammals, from small mice and voles, through medium-sized deer, wild pigs, and goats, to large zebras, antelopes, and gazelles. In the Age of Dinosaurs the ornithopods – the "bird-footed" dinosaurs – were reptilian versions of these grazers and browsers. They were among the most numerous and varied herbivores of the time.

The best-known animals of the African plains are perhaps the lions, leopards, and other big cats, and the huge plant-eaters such as elephants, rhinos, and giraffes. But by far the most numerous large animals are the antelopes, gazelles, zebras, gnus, and other herbivores.

There were many herbivores living in the Age of Dinosaurs too. They belonged mainly to the dinosaur group called ornithopods. They are called "bird-footed" because their feet and toes resembled those of today's birds. They were the "standard herbivores" of the time.

Groups of ornithopods

The ornithopods included:

- fabrosaurs such as *Lesothosaurus* or *Fabrosaurus*, although they can also be viewed as an earlier and separate group;
- heterodontosaurs, including *Heterodontosaurus*;
- hypsilophodonts such as *Hypsilophodon*;
- dryosaurs such as *Dryosaurus*;
- camptosaurs, including *Camptosaurus*;
- iguanodonts, especially one of the best-known of all dinosaurs, *Iguanodon*, and also the sail-backed *Ouranosaurus*;
- hadrosaurs, or "duck-billed" dinosaurs, which are a large and fascinating subgroup in their own right, and are covered separately in volume 9 of this series.

This book describes these and other members of the Ornithopoda group. They lived at various times through almost the entire Age of Dinosaurs, from about 200 million years ago to the great extinction of all dinosaurs 65 million years ago.

Herbivores then and now

Herds of herbivores such as deer browse peacefully in our woodlands today. In dinosaur times, these mammals had not yet evolved. Instead there were ornithopod dinosaurs chewing leaves and wandering among the trees.

▲ **White-tailed deer – a browser**
Deer are among the most numerous of large herbivores found today. They are woodland browsers, like some of their reptilian equivalents in the Age of the Dinosaurs.

◄ **Early dinosaur models**
The types of ornithopods called iguanodonts, in the shape of *Iguanodon* itself, were some of the first dinosaurs to be studied and named by scientists. And these nineteenth-century lifesized versions constructed for the gardens of London's Crystal Palace were some of the first models to be made of any dinosaur. However, our ideas about dinosaurs have changed greatly since, and the models are now regarded as fascinating but inaccurate historical curiosities (see also page 17).

What were the ornithopods?

The dinosaurs known as ornithopods, group Ornithopoda, were a subgroup of a much larger group of dinosaurs — the Ornithischia, or "bird-hips." Other members of the Ornithischia included:

- the plated dinosaurs or stegosaurs, with upright plates of bone along their backs;
- the armored dinosaurs, or ankylosaurs, with massive bony plates like shields in their skin;
- the bone-headed dinosaurs, or pachycephalosaurs, with thick crests or helmets of bone on their heads;
- the horned dinosaurs or ceratopsians, with long horns on their heads and bony frills over their necks.

The Ornithischia, which were all plant-eaters, made up one of the two great groups of dinosaurs.

The other great group was the Saurischians, or "lizard-hips." It included all meat-eating dinosaurs, the theropods, from huge *Tyrannosaurus*, through medium-sized *Deinonychus* and *Velociraptor*, to tiny *Compsognathus*. It also included the largest of all dinosaurs, the sauropods — small-headed, long-necked, barrel-bodied, long-tailed, pillar-legged giants such as *Brachiosaurus* and *Diplodocus*.

The Saurischia and Ornithischia together made up the group of reptiles we call Dinosauria, or "terrible lizards" — the dinosaurs.

This series covers all of the above-mentioned dinosaur groups and also the creatures that lived alongside the dinosaurs on land and in the air and water all those millions of years ago.

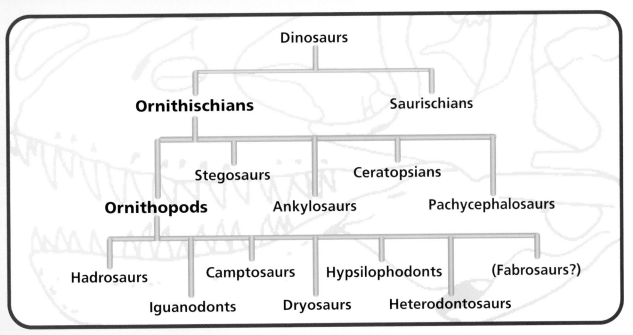

→ The early ornithopods

The ornithopods were one of the biggest and ecologically most important of all dinosaur groups. Not only widespread, they were also varied in size and shape and commonly attacked by dinosaur predators.

The ornithopods ("bird-footed"), a subgroup of the Ornithischia ("bird-hipped") dinosaurs, varied vastly in size and shape. They followed different lifestyles – although all were plant-eaters. Members of the group persisted through most of the Age of Dinosaurs, becoming especially common in the Cretaceous Period (144-65 million years ago). They also spread to most parts of the prehistoric world.

Evolution and ecology

The ornithopods were important in several ways. They may have been the ancestors of the other groups of ornithischian dinosaurs such as pachycephalosaurs, ceratopsians, stegosaurs, and ankylosaurs. Because they were so abundant they were regularly hunted for food by larger dinosaurs, or eaten dead by the scavengers of the time. So ornithopods played many roles in the food chains and ecology of the dinosaur world.

Early evolution of ornithopods

Where did the ornithopods come from? We do not know for sure, but their ancestors may have been small, meat-eating reptiles known as thecodonts (see volume 1 of this series). A possible "halfway" version may have been a very early ornithischian, *Pisanosaurus*, from the Late Triassic Period. Its fossils have been found in Argentina (see page 46).

Not quite ornithopods?

Another possibility is that ornithopods were descended from fabrosaurs. They were another Late Triassic group, but their remains are scarce and incomplete. In fact, it is not even certain that they formed a distinct group. They may just be a "trashcan" collection of unrelated dinosaurs, which scientists have bunched together for convenience. Some of them may have been ancestral to the ornithopods. They may not. Fabrosaurs were small, speedy creatures that ran mainly on their two back legs. They lived on well into the Jurassic Period (see pages 40-43).

First ornithopods

The first clear members of the ornithopod group were the heterodontosaurs. They are named from their teeth, which had different shapes and jobs in different parts of the mouth. Our own teeth are like this, but for reptiles in general this is an unusual feature. Crocodiles, for example, tend to have very similar teeth all along the jaws. The heterodontosaurs lived mainly during the Early Jurassic Period in Africa and Asia. Like

◄ A very early ornithischian
A small *Pisanosaurus*, possibly one of the earliest of the heterodont dinosaurs, walks through a Late Triassic forest. The air is full of fern and other plant spores.

fabrosaurs, they were little, agile, and bipedal (running on two legs).

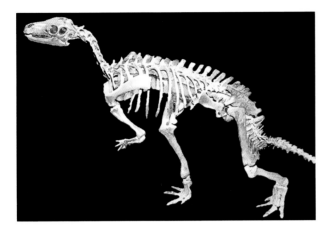

▲ An early small ornithopod
Computer enhancement adds clarity to this image of a fossilized *Camptosaurus* skeleton. *Camptosaurus* was one of the earliest members of the iguanodontids group, smaller and more primitive than most of that family (see page 28).

Small ornithopods
The hypsilophodonts were a longlived ornithopod group that spread around the world. They too were small, speedy bipeds, with five-fingered hands and four-toed feet. The beaklike mouth contained front upper biting teeth and rear upper and lower chewing teeth.

Medium and larger ornithopods
The dryosaurs resembled medium-sized versions of *Iguanodon*. Their fossils have been found in North America, Europe, Africa, and New Zealand. Each had three toes on each foot and a toothless, beaklike mouth.

The camptosaurs were larger still – heavily built dinosaurs from the second half of the Jurassic Period, found around the world.

> **Main features of the ornithopods**
> * A birdlike hipbone, or pelvis. (This is the single most important feature by which all ornithischian dinosaurs can be identified.)
> * An extra bone at the tip of the lower jaw, with a horny, beaklike covering.
> * A trellislike arrangement of bony ligaments supporting the backbone.
> * In most types a bone in the eye socket called the palpebral bone. Its function is still unclear.
> * Early ornithopods were mostly small, only a few feet long, lightly built and agile.
> * They were bipedal — they walked and ran on their two larger back legs, holding the two smaller front legs off the ground like "arms."
> * Later ornithopods were much bigger and more heavily built, the size of a car or small truck, with larger front legs.
> * However, they probably still mostly ran on two legs.

They had close-packed grinding teeth and feet with four hoofed toes.

Advanced ornithopods
The iguanodontids were large, heavy dinosaurs, walking on two or four feet. The rear feet each had three hoofed toes. The fingers too had hooves and a spiked thumb. These dinosaurs lived all over the world for the whole of the Cretaceous Period.

(The very advanced ornithopods known as the hadrosaurs are described in volume 9 of the series.)

◄ A runner on two legs?
This skeleton of *Iguanodon* is mounted in the pose it could have adopted in life — standing on its two back legs and holding its front legs like arms.

The finding of *Iguanodon* ➤

The finding of *Iguanodon*

Iguanodon was probably the second kind of dinosaur to be discovered and described in a scientific way – even before the word "dinosaur" itself had been made up!

Iguanodon is one of the best-known members, not only of the ornithopods, but of the whole dinosaur group. Fossils from hundreds of individuals have been discovered, along with trace fossils such as trackways and droppings (see page 37). From this evidence we can reconstruct *Iguanodon* and recreate its lifestyle in more detail and with more confidence than we can for almost any other dinosaur.

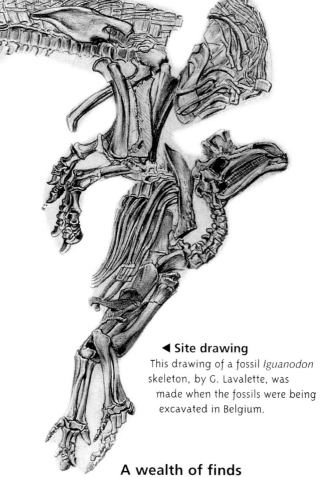

Doubtful beginnings

The first known *Iguanodon* fossils were probably a shinbone found in southern England in 1809 and some teeth in 1819. The animal was reconstructed in 1822 and in 1825 it was named by Gideon Mantell, a physician and fossil hunter (see page 16).

When fossils from around 39 individuals were discovered in a mine at Bernissart in Belgium in 1878, more accurate reconstructions of this mysterious beast could be made. Experts of the day began to think of *Iguanodon* standing in a kangaroolike posture and having a spike on its thumb. Further changes in our ideas about this dinosaur are shown on pages 16-17.

◄ **Site drawing**
This drawing of a fossil *Iguanodon* skeleton, by G. Lavalette, was made when the fossils were being excavated in Belgium.

Exposing fossils

Iguanodon fossils are now known from dozens of sites in Europe and Asia, where rocks of the Early to Middle Cretaceous Period lie at or near the surface. Fossils usually come to light when rocks are exposed or worn away by the action of the rain, wind, and sun. This occurs especially in areas such as the Badlands of the U.S., the Australian outback, the African savanna, the Gobi Desert in Asia, and the pampas of South America.

In Europe such harsh conditions are rare. Fossils, including those of *Iguanodon*, are more likely to be exposed by the actions of people at building sites, quarries, and mines or perhaps by the action of the sea along rocky coasts.

A wealth of finds

This is why particularly rich sites for *Iguanodon* fossils include the rocks and quarries of the Weald in southeast England, a quarry at Nehden in Germany, and the mine at Bernissart. From the numbers of remains it is thought that *Iguanodon* was a very common animal across the lowlands of Europe during the Early to Middle Cretaceous Period.

Fragmentary remains that may or may not be *Iguanodon*, along with fossilized footprints possibly made by this dinosaur, have been found in Africa, North and South America, and Australia.

British *Iguanodon*

The Wealden fossils of *Iguanodon* were mostly scattered over an area that was once a fertile, lowland plain, crisscrossed by streams and rivers. As the dinosaurs died, their remains were washed into the rivers, perhaps by heavy rain or by floods coming down from higher ground.

The carcasses rotted, and the bones became separated as they were rolled around in the water. Occasionally a more complete specimen is found, which is articulated – the fossil bones are still in position and next to each other at their joints, as they were in life. One specimen from near Hastings was probably an *Iguanodon* that fell into a swamp or lake and was rapidly buried in clay before its skeleton fell apart.

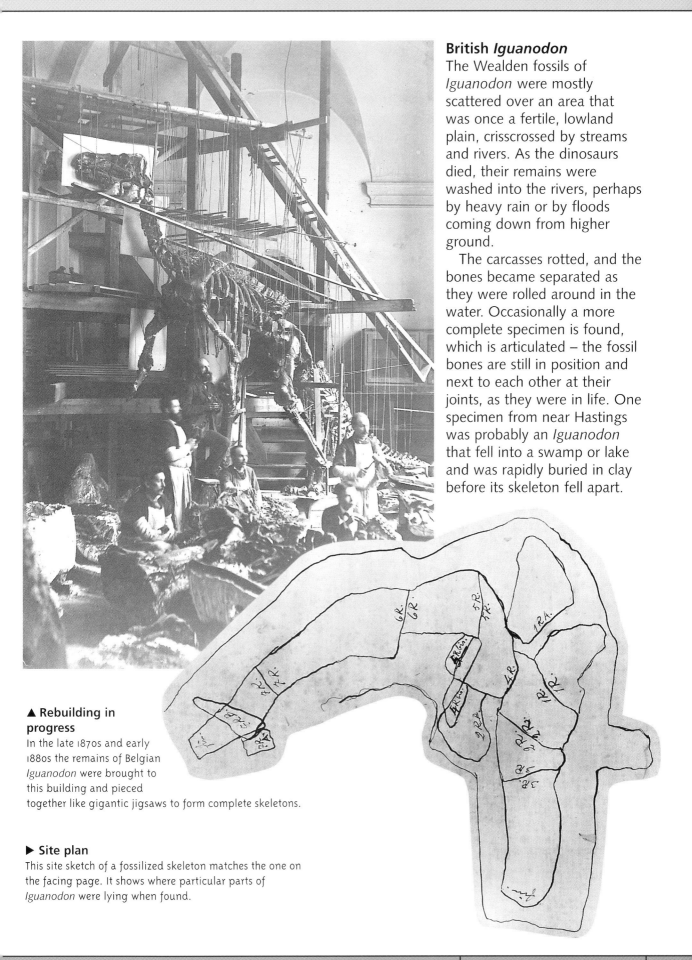

▲ Rebuilding in progress

In the late 1870s and early 1880s the remains of Belgian *Iguanodon* were brought to this building and pieced together like gigantic jigsaws to form complete skeletons.

▶ Site plan

This site sketch of a fossilized skeleton matches the one on the facing page. It shows where particular parts of *Iguanodon* were lying when found.

⇨ Reconstructing *Iguanodon*

Putting *Iguanodon* together has been easy thanks to an abundance of bones found at several sites.

▲ Together at last
This *Iguanodon* skeleton was laid out in the position in which it was discovered.

Belgian *Iguanodon*

In 1878 a clay-filled crack or fissure was discovered running through a coal mine at Bernissart, about 1,000 feet (300 meters) below the surface. The clay was packed with fossilized whole skeletons of about 39 *Iguanodon*, as well as remains of many other animals and plants of the time.

The rocks bearing the skeletons were broken into manageable lumps and sent to the laboratory of the Natural History Museum in Brussels. Before the lumps were removed from the mine, the position of each skeleton was carefully recorded. So were the nature and condition of the surrounding rock. Every piece had its own reference number. The skeletons could therefore be assembled much more easily. Sadly, the First World War made further excavation impossible. The Bernissart mine was abandoned in 1921 and soon flooded.

Hand and finger bones
The bones of *Iguanodon*'s fingers have many details that allow accurate reconstruction. The joints between the thumb bones show that this first digit was probably almost rigid. The three middle fingers could bend backward to take weight. The joints of the fifth or little finger were extremely flexible. The dinosaur could probably bend it across the palm to grasp objects — rather like our own thumb, but on the other side of the hand (digit five rather than digit one).

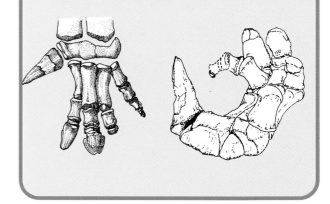

◄ The finding of *Iguanodon*

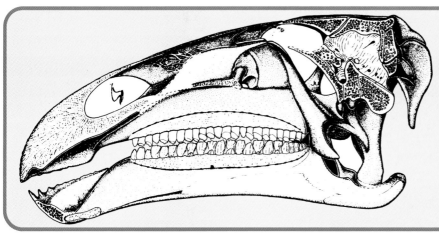

Skull
Iguanodon had long, horselike jaws, and the end of the mouth formed a toothless beak. This was probably covered with sharp-edged horn. The 100 or so cheek teeth grew in parallel rows, forming a continuous platform for grinding food.

German *Iguanodon*

Scattered bone fragments found in clay at the abandoned Nehden quarry stimulated a major excavation of the site in 1980-82. The site was divided up into a grid and a map made. Then the remains were removed layer by layer. This method produced an excellent three-dimensional picture of the remains. At first glance, if you looked at the usual overhead view, the bones seemed to be scattered at random. But the full three-dimensional record showed that the skeletons, including that of a youngster, were lying vertically in the clay.

Reconstructing *Iguanodon*

The great number and variety of *Iguanodon* fossils make the task of reconstruction relatively straightforward.

The skeleton itself is known from many well-preserved and articulated specimens. Muscle scars, roughened patches where muscles were anchored to the bones, can be clearly seen. In turn, this information shows the size and arrangement of the muscles and how they worked in the hips, back legs, shoulders, arms, and jaws. In building up the picture of the way the muscles joined on to bones, comparative anatomy is important. Comparisons are made with the muscle systems of other, related animals, especially living reptiles. Other evidence for the leg musculature comes from fossilized footprints or trackways, which reveal how *Iguanodon* walked and ran (see page 20).

DATA BASE

Name	*Iguanodon*
Pronounced	Ig-WAH-no-don
Meaning	"iguana tooth"

What it ate Plant-eater, feeding on rich swamp vegetation such as horsetails, ferns, cycads, bennettileans, and small conifers

Length	(nose - tail-tip) 30 feet (9.1 meters)
Standing height	14 feet (4.3 meters)
Weight	5 tons (5.1 tonnes)

When it lived	Early to Middle Cretaceous Period 135-110 million years ago
Where it lived	Europe (England, Belgium, Germany, Spain), Africa (Tunisia), Asia (Mongolia), North America (South Dakota, U.S.)

Order	Ornithischia (bird-hipped dinosaurs)
Suborder	Ornithopoda
Family	Iguanodontidae

A dinosaur's brain? ▶

⇨ A dinosaur's brain?

Most fossils are of hard parts such as bones, teeth, claws, and horns. But occasionally fossils show the size and shape of a soft body part – even a brain.

The vast majority of fossils, including those of dinosaurs, take thousands or even millions of years to form. They are the hardest, toughest parts of the organism, which resist rotting, scavenger attack, weathering, and erosion. They become buried in the ground. Groundwater soaking through the layers of the ground carries natural minerals, which gradually, molecule by molecule, replace the substance of these animal parts.

Bone to stone
This process, called permineralization, turns "bone to stone." Fossils are not simply the original objects hardened and preserved. They have the shapes of the original objects but they are made from solid rock. If this happens slowly with little or no disturbance of the sediments, the fossil is exactly like what was there originally – right down to the microscopic structure.

▲ A jumble of bones
These bones of *Iguanodon* are part of a collection that came from Maidstone, Kent, England.

◄ The brain of *Iguanodon*
The *Iguanodon* find shows that for a reptile, the brain was large in relation to the body. The brain was big enough not only to process the input signals from the eyes, ears, and other sense organs but also to deal with complex social behavior. In this endocast fossil (side view) the nerves and vessels joining to the brain can be seen as short stumps on the right.

◄ ▶ *Iguanodon* with ailments
The bone (left) shows muscle scars where muscles were attached to it. On the right is a middle toe with an arthritic joint shown by the bony ridge running across about halfway up.

Filling in
Sometimes the original material, such as a bone or tooth, rots or dissolves away before permineralization occurs. Then a space or empty hole, with the shape of the original object is left in the sediments. It may gradually fill with other minerals. The resulting fossil has two parts. The hole left in the rock – which surrounds an empty space – is called a mold fossil. Whatever has filled the hole is called a cast fossil.

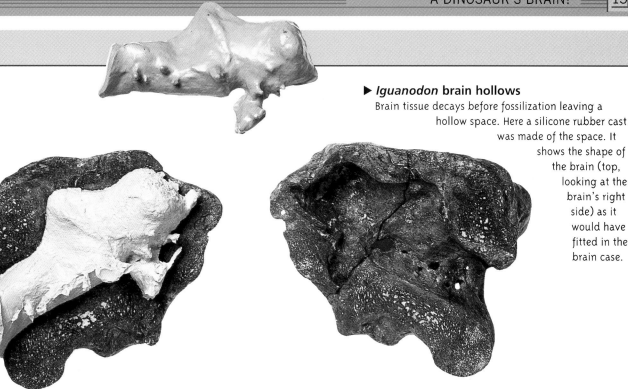

▶ *Iguanodon* brain hollows
Brain tissue decays before fossilization leaving a hollow space. Here a silicone rubber cast was made of the space. It shows the shape of the brain (top, looking at the brain's right side) as it would have fitted in the brain case.

Inside the skull

Mold and cast fossils can take on the shapes and surface features of the soft organs and tissues that originally filled the hole.

One damaged fossil skull specimen of *Iguanodon* was found lying near a piece of rock that turned out to be an endocast (internal cast) of the animal's brain. It showed the shape and surface details of the brain itself. Not only were its shape and surface details clear but also the main nerves running from the brain out to the head and body, the brain's blood vessels, the inner ear structure, and even the size and shape of the tiny pituitary gland just below the brain. This gland is an organ that makes hormones, which are chemical messengers that control many bodily processes.

▶ Skilled defense
Iguanodon may have used its sharp-clawed "hands" in self-defense against large predators such as the carnosaur-type dinosaurs like *Megalosaurus*. *Iguanodon* had a fairly large brain that controlled its complex behavior.

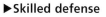

⇨ Early ideas about *Iguanodon*

Science progresses as we devise new equipment, refine our methods and techniques, and increase our understanding. A look back at early reconstructions of *Iguanodon* illustrates this progress in action.

The discoverer of *Iguanodon's* fossils was physician Gideon Mantell (1790-1852). He was based at Lewes in Sussex, southern England. Today, we know a vast amount about fossils, prehistory, evolution, classification, and the dinosaurs themselves, and can slot new discoveries into an existing framework. In Mantell's day the scientific world was very different.

A different world

In the early nineteenth century scientists were struggling to accept the idea that the animals and plants they knew were not the only species that had ever existed on earth. Fossils were known and suspected to be the remains of once-living things. But they were thought to be recently dead creatures or giant humans drowned in the Great Flood described in the Bible.

In about 1770 the fossils of *Mosasaurus*, a giant marine lizard from the Age of Dinosaurs, came to light in a chalk quarry in Maastricht, Netherlands. They were unlike the parts of any living creature and were described in detail by the eminent comparative anatomist Georges Cuvier (1769-1832). The fossils provided extremely strong evidence that other, quite different species had lived long ago on earth, and had become extinct. Scientists began bravely to tackle such ideas, which went against the teachings of the Church and popular opinion.

▲Teeth
Above are some of the original *Iguanodon* teeth found by Dr and Mrs Mantell. The curved tooth on the right is 2 inches (5.4 cm) Long.

◄A kangaroolike animal
In the 1880s Louis Dollo used the kangaroo — a large bipedal animal with a heavy tail — as a model for reconstructing *Iguanodon*. The pose stuck for many decades.

Extinct rhinoceros?

Gideon Mantell (or possibly his wife) discovered the first *Iguanodon* teeth at a gravel roadwork site. Mantell was a keen amateur geologist and had studied biology as part of his medical training. From his knowledge of living creatures and the age of the rocks in the quarry he identified the fossil teeth as reptilian.

Mantell had the teeth and other remains studied by geologists who also understood anatomy, including William Buckland in Oxford and Georges Cuvier himself in Paris. They were unimpressed and said that the remains could come from a large mammal or even a fish that had died quite recently. Cuvier suggested an extinct type of rhinoceros.

History Museum in London, commissioned sculptor Benjamin Waterhouse Hawkins to make models of the great beasts for the grounds of Crystal Palace when it moved to south London after the Great Exhibition of 1850-51 in Hyde Park. These life-sized, brick-and-concrete models were the first reconstructions of dinosaurs and can still be seen at the old Crystal Palace site in Sydenham, south London.

◀ Like a lizard
This model of *Iguanodon*, made in the 1850s by Waterhouse Hawkins, shows the lizardlike posture that scientists used to think was accurate. The model stands in a park in south London.

◀ Bolt upright?
Scientists now think that *Iguanodon*'s tail curved less and its backbone was more horizontal than in the model pictured in this colored engraving. It shows visitors viewing *Iguanodon* in a museum in 1883.

◀ Skeleton under the vaults
Iguanodon was reconstructed in the medieval — but not prehistoric — Chapel of St Georges in Brussels in 1879 or

The lizard phase
Soon after, a chance meeting with an expert on Central American lizards showed that the fossil teeth Mantell had found were like the teeth of the living lizard called the iguana, although much larger. In 1822 Mantell published a description of the fossils and his version of the reconstructed animal. He calculated it would have been huge, 40 feet (12.2 meters) long. He pictured it like a modern lizard, walking on all four limbs, which sprawled out sideways, and with a heavy tail dragging behind.

One of the fossil fragments was a strange, bony spike. Perhaps thinking of Cuvier's rhinoceros theory, Mantell suggested that it might have been on the animal's nose. In 1825 he formally named the beast *Iguanodon*, "iguana-tooth."

Dinosaurs come alive
In 1841 anatomist Richard Owen coined the name "dinosaur" for a new reptile group to include *Iguanodon*, the meat-eater *Megalosaurus*, and other discoveries. Owen, who became superintendent of the Natural

The kangaroo phase
In 1878 many specimens of *Iguanodon* were discovered in a Belgian mine (see page 12). They provided excellent material for newer reconstructions by Louis Dollo from the 1880s to the 1920s.

One large bipedal animal with a heavy tail known to Dollo was the kangaroo. So he stood *Iguanodon* more upright on its back legs, and propped it up at the rear with its tail (breaking the bones to get the tail into the correct angle). He also moved the body spike from the nose onto the thumb.

Dollo believed the bones of the foot could work as grasping toes. So, according to him, *Iguanodon* was a giant, 5-ton (5.1 tonne) tree-kangaroo (but we have to wonder what tree had strong enough branches to support such a beast!).

⇒ Life and times of *iguanodon*

Modern methods of analysis, looking at so many different aspects of Iguanodon, from the relative size of the sexes to the detail of wear on fossil teeth, reveal the structure, lifestyle, and ecology of this dinosaur.

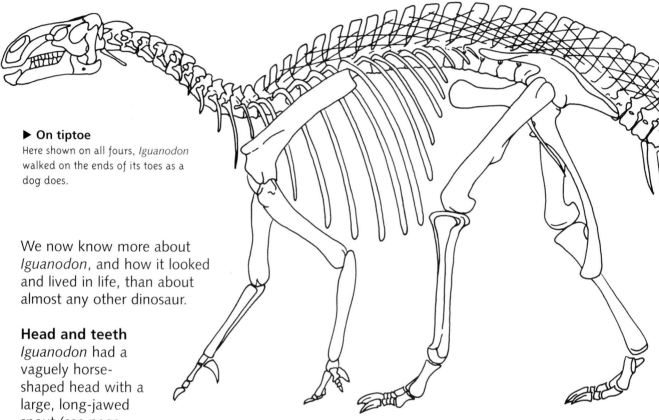

▶ On tiptoe
Here shown on all fours, *Iguanodon* walked on the ends of its toes as a dog does.

We now know more about *Iguanodon*, and how it looked and lived in life, than about almost any other dinosaur.

Head and teeth
Iguanodon had a vaguely horse-shaped head with a large, long-jawed snout (see page 13). The jaws ended in a toothless, horny beak that probably had irregular or serrated edges, like the mouth of a turtle or tortoise, for chopping leaves.

The teeth pointed slightly away from the outer sides of the jaws. This created space on their outsides for cheek pouches of skin.

Feeding
A line of looser joints between bones of the skull formed a hinge that ran diagonally across each side of the face, from just behind the beak, across the eye socket,

▶ A reptilian giraffe?
Iguanodon might have reached up with its long neck to feed on high vegetation, as a giraffe does today.

to the upper rear of the skull. It allowed the bones of the upper jaw to move apart and the lower jaw to rise between them. It meant the upper and lower cheek teeth rubbed past each other while chewing to grind the food and also to sharpen each other.

Strong, elastic straps called ligaments spanned the joints in the skull and jaws. They allowed the joints to flex and spring back during eating, absorbing stresses and saving energy. There was also a pronglike extension at the lower rear of the mandible (lower jawbone), facing the neck. A muscle attached to this would give the jaws greater leverage for even better chewing.

Front limbs

Iguanodon's long, thick arms each ended in five fingers (see page 12). The wrist and palm bones were strong and firmly bound or fused together for bearing weight but limited movement.

The central three fingers could splay out backward to support the weight of the upper body, although they could not curl inward to grasp. These middle fingers were tipped with hooves rather than claws. The fifth finger formed a small, flexible grasping hook. The rigid thumb had a large, straight claw or spike and stuck out at right angles to the hand.

What was the thumb-spike for?

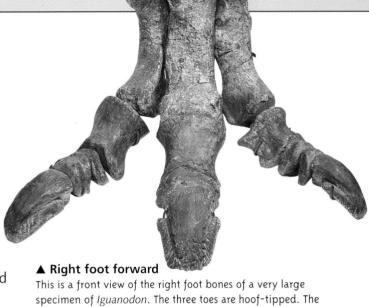

▲ Right foot forward
This is a front view of the right foot bones of a very large specimen of *Iguanodon*. The three toes are hoof-tipped. The general similarity of this foot structure to that of a bird led to the name ornithopod "bird foot."

Raking vegetation near the mouth, perhaps. Jabbing at enemies, possibly (see page 15). Sexual display? For holding a partner while mating, even? No one is sure.

Rear limbs

The pillarlike legs of *Iguanodon* ended in relatively big feet, each with three hoof-tipped toes. The dinosaur walked on the ends of these toes, like a dog. This kind of walk is called digitigrade posture. In the plantigrade posture animals walk on their palms and soles, with the fingers out to the front or side, like bears.

Today the perissodactyls, or odd-toed ungulates, are hoofed mammals with three toes per foot, such as rhinos and tapirs.

Once a thing of mystery
Early paleontologists thought this spike must have been on *Iguanodon*'s nose. We now assume that it was attached to the thumb.

◄ Big feet
Rough patches on this metatarsal, a bone running the length of the foot, are muscle scars, where muscles and tendons were attached to it.

⇨ Lifestyle of *Iguanodon*

Iguanodon was large and powerful but probably lived peacefully unless attacked.

Posture

Modern reconstructions of *Iguanodon* picture the dinosaur standing on its two back legs, main body horizontal, to counterbalance the weight of the head and upper body in front with the large tail behind. The neck is bent in a shallow S shape to raise the head, and the tail is held out rigidly behind.

A feature of the ornithopods is a vertebral column, or backbone, in which large projections of bone from the upper vertebrae are bound tightly together by lengthways bony tendons. This stiffened the backbone and made it look like a length of grid fencing (see opposite). Perhaps

Iguanodon could tilt its body up at its hips, lowering its tail for balance, to browse on higher vegetation. Or it could lean forward and take the weight of the upper body on its front legs when walking on all fours or browsing on low vegetation. But it was unable to bend the main part of its backbone much or to prop itself on its tail like a kangaroo.

Movement

Iguanodon had a small, irregular-shaped bone in its chest, which few other dinosaurs had. It may have evolved to cope with the physical stresses imposed on the chest when moving on all fours.

The relative lengths of the upper and lower leg bones, when compared with those of living animals, give clues about dinosaur posture and movement. Modern fast runners such as gazelles

▲ A formidable herbivore

Iguanodon was no small and timid plant-eater. A predator would have had trouble overcoming it. The thumb with its spike was almost 12 inches (30.5 cm) long. However, we have very few fossils of large predators in Europe dating from the Early to Middle Cretaceous Period. Was this lack of carnivores one reason why *Iguanodon* were so plentiful?

▲ Herbivore herd-dwellers
Zebras are peaceful herbivores, which live in herds as
Iguanodon probably did .

Male and female?
Specimens of *Iguanodon* that have attained full adult
size, as shown by the body proportions and bone
development, seem to fall into two groups. There are
large, heavy ones and there are smaller, more lightly
built individuals.

They could have been two distinct species, but it is
unlikely. The study of ecology today shows that two
such similar species, living at the same time and in the
same place, would be competing directly for food and
other resources.

Another explanation is that these two groups represent
two sexes, male and female. In modern mammals, the
males are usually larger. But in modern reptiles, such as
crocodiles and snakes, the females are sometimes
bigger. The evidence from *Iguanodon* fossils does not
tell us for certain which is which.

and cheetahs have bones in the shin and foot,
that are proportionally longer than the bones
in the upper leg. The bulky muscles that move
the bones are concentrated in the hip and
upper thigh, while the lower leg contains only
lightweight bones and long, slim tendons. This
is the condition found in the ornithopod
Dryosaurus (see pages 30-31).

Iguanodon, on the other hand, had fairly
long thighs compared with the shins and feet.
This implies it was not a rapid sprinter but
would pound along at perhaps 8-10 miles per
hour
(13-16 km/h).

Lifestyle
The place that an animal occupies in its
environment – where and how it lives – is
called its ecological niche. For example,
sharks and tigers are top predators
today. In the Age of Dinosaurs

Allosaurus and *Tyrannosaurus* probably played
that part.

Iguanodon may well have filled a niche
equivalent to modern wild horses and zebras
or large antelopes. They lived in large herds
(see pages 36-37), peacefully wandering
through the tropical forests and scrublands.
They could reach up perhaps 15 feet (4.6
meters) for high vegetation or flop
down onto all fours to
graze on low-growing
ferns and horsetails.

Trellis backbone
These are ossified, or bony, tendons. They are bands of
fibrous tissue attaching muscles to bones. A trellis or
grid pattern of such tendons along the upper flangelike
projections of the backbones is a typical feature of
ornithopod dinosaurs.

 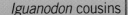

Iguanodon cousins

The ornithopod family Iguanodontidae contained several smallish and medium-sized plant-eating dinosaurs.

The iguanodontids, to which *Iguanodon* of course belongs, are one of the best-known families of ornithopod dinosaurs. Fossil evidence shows that they first appeared in the Late Jurassic Period, some 150 million years ago, with types such as *Callovosaurus*. They probably evolved from hypsilophodon-type ancestors, but the iguanodontids existed alongside the hypsilophodontids in many areas, specializing in different types of food to avoid direct competition.

Rising to a peak

The iguanodontids spread all over the world, even to the Arctic Circle – which would not have been so cold then. Also, the landmasses would have had different shapes from the present ones because of continental drift, the movement of the continents on the earth's crust. In fact, the spread of iguanodontids across the continents tells us a lot about where the continents were and how they were linked at the time. This family of dinosaurs was most varied and widespread during the Early Cretaceous Period.

Fading away

The iguanodontids gradually declined during the Middle to Late Cretaceous Period. This was possibly due to the rise of another ornithopod group, the hadrosaurs. They flourished especially in North America and Asia, and probably fed on similar food to the iguanodontids, so they were direct competitors. However, it seems that hadrosaurs never became especially numerous in western Europe or southern landmasses such as Africa because of the gaps between the continents. Iguanodontids such as *Kangnasaurus* (which in any case may have been a dryosaur or heterodontosaur) and *Mochlodon* did survive in the Late Cretaceous Period in western Europe and Africa.

▼ **Danger alert**
An iguanodontid in a forest clearing (left) turns its head, sensing the danger from a *Megalosaurus*-type predatory dinosaur nearby (right).

The iguanodontids *Muttaburrasaurus*, *Ouranosaurus*, and *Camptosaurus* are featured on the following pages. Other types are described here.

> **Family features**
> The typical features of the iguanodontids included:
> * a bulky, heavy body;
> * longer thighs than shins, indicating that they moved relatively slowly;
> * large hands, more adapted for walking on all fours than for manipulating food;
> * wide, weight-bearing feet;
> * fingers and toes with heavy hooves rather than nails or claws, again suited to moving on all fours;
> * long, horselike skull and jaws;
> * a toothless, horny beak at the front of the mouth for nipping and snipping off plant food;
> * rows of closely packed, high-ridged cheek teeth for cutting and grinding the food.

Callovosaurus

The main fossil of the "Callovian lizard" from the Middle Jurassic rocks of England is a single, damaged thighbone. But it is enough to suggest it was an early iguanodontid rather than a hypsilophodontid, with a total body length of almost 12 feet (3.7 meters). However, the bone was slender, so *Callovosaurus* might have been a hypsilophodont, perhaps a type of dryosaur (see page 30).

Vectisaurus

The "Isle of Wight lizard" dates from the Early Cretaceous Period of England. It was about 13 feet (4 meters) long and very similar to *Iguanodon*. It also lived in the same region at about the same time as *Iguanodon* and so could have been another species of the overall genus. But it also had long spines along its backbone, as did the "sail-backed" iguanodontid, *Ouranosaurus* (see pages 26-27).

Mochlodon, also known as Rhabdodon

"Bar tooth" or "rod tooth" describes the tooth shape of this iguanodontid, one of the latest survivors of the family. It was bipedal and relatively small, about 13 feet (4 meters) long, with both iguanodontid and hysilophodontid features. Its fossils are about 70-65 million years old, from the Late Cretaceous Period, and have been uncovered in Spain, France, Austria, and Romania.

Probactrosaurus

Another Middle-Late Cretaceous type, "pre-Bactrian lizard" is known from fossils in Mongolia and China. They show a 20-foot (6.1-meter), bipedal or quadrupedal iguanodontid. It may have survived the rising success of the "duckbill" hadrosaurs because it was isolated geographically from them. Interestingly, *Probactrosaurus* was very much like *Iguanodon*, yet had some hadrosaur features too. This may mean it was a descendant of the hadrosaurs or even an early member of this group of ornithopods.

Fossil footprint
This is a trace fossil — not the remains of an actual body part, but of a telltale sign left behind. These types of prints reveal a lot. We can estimate the weight of the dinosaur from their depth and its stride length and so walking or running speed from the distance between successive prints. The coin at the top gives an idea of scale, the whole print being about 12 inches (30 cm) long (see also page 36).

→ *Muttaburrasaurus* and its lump

Muttaburrasaurus, with a bulge on its nose, is one of the growing number of dinosaurs known from fossils recovered in Australia.

The fossils of *Muttaburrasaurus* were unearthed in the grassy, subtropical plains of central Queensland state, in northeastern Australia. It was a dinosaur very similar in size and shape to *Iguanodon* itself, as described below. But it had one distinctive feature. It was a bony lump or bulge in the upper snout area, between the nostrils.

Why a bump on the nose?

Muttaburrasaurus was not the only dinosaur that had such a lumpy nose. Another ornithopod had one. But it was a hadrosaur and not an iguanodontid. It was *Kritosaurus*. Ideas put forward to explain the presence of the lump are similar for both types.

- Was it to increase the size of the cavity in the nose for a better sense of smell for finding food?
- Was it covered with thickened skin possibly as a weapon?
- Was it covered with some type of gristle, which did not

Australian dinosaur
Muttaburrasaurus remains have been found in northeastern Australia. It is named after the place where they were found.

fossilize, again as a weapon, but which made the bump larger?

- Or was it the base for an inflatable bag of skin that could be blown up like a balloon?
- Did only one sex have it to allow recognition of the opposite sex at mating time?

▲ *Iguanodon* with a lump
Muttaburrasaurus had a toothless, horny turtle-beak at the front of its mouth, similar to *Iguanodon*'s. Its remains are not complete enough or well-preserved enough to show its hand bones in detail, but again, they seem similar to those of *Iguanodon*, with four main fingers and a spiny or spiky thumb.

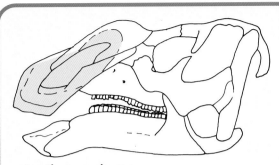

Another nosebump
The skull of the hadrosaur *Kritosaurus* also bears a lump on the nose. A modern animal that has an inflatable nose is the elephant seal.

separated geographically– develop such similar features? As usual, there are several possibilities.

- Perhaps the same feature evolved independently in each type to cope with similar conditions or pressures of life. When the same development happens in different species and in different environments, it is known as convergent evolution.
- Maybe the two types descended from a single ancestor that had the nose lump. The two descendant types then migrated away from each other. But this would involve a very long migration, given the way the continents were laid out at the time.

- Was it a symbol of maturity for one or both sexes? That would have meant that these reptiles did not waste energy trying to mate with an immature individual.
- Was it for display, to protect a territory from invaders or strangers?

Oriental connections

No other iguanodontid dinosaur possessed a large nose lump, or crest, like *Muttaburrasaurus*. Except, that is, for the Mongolian species in the same genus as *Iguanodon*, named *Iguanodon orientalis*. It lived at about the same time but in eastern Asia. But why should these two types – closely related in terms of evolution but widely

Cutting teeth
Compared with the cheek teeth of *Iguanodon*, those of *Muttaburrasaurus* were more suited to cutting than to grinding. They probably operated more like sets of tough scissors or the blade of a food processor rather than as crushers and grinders.

Nose lump

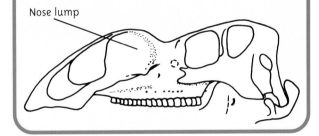

DATA BASE

Name *Muttaburrasaurus*
Pronounced MUTT-a-BURRAH-sore-us
Meaning "Muttaburra lizard"

What it ate
Plants of various kinds, including conifers

Length (nose - tail-tip) 24 feet (7.3 meters)
Standing height 16 feet (4.9 meters)
Weight 1-2 tons (1-2 tonnes)

When it lived Early Cretaceous Period 140 million years ago
Where it lived Australia (Queensland)

Order Ornithischia (bird-hipped dinosaurs)
Suborder Ornithopoda
Family Iguanodontidae

Ouranosaurus sets sail ▶

Ouranosaurus sets sail

"Sail-backed" animals have come and gone many times during evolution. Among them were various reptiles, including a few types of dinosaurs, such as the *Iguanodon*-type ornithopod *Ouranosaurus*.

Ouranosaurus is one of the best-known of the "sail-backed" dinosaurs. They had fin- or saillike structures on their backs. The sail was probably a thin sheet of muscle and connective tissue sandwiched between skin. It was held up by tall, stiff, straplike bones called neural spines, each projecting from one of the vertebrae (backbones). In *Ouranosaurus* the longest of these projections were about 3 feet (1 meter) long.

Several other kinds of dinosaurs had such huge, saillike structures on their backs. They included the carnosaur *Spinosaurus* (see opposite) and the sauropod *Rebbachisaurus*. Shoulders and flanks were protected by long, sharp spines pointing forward and sideways.

Similar to *Iguanodon*

The fossils of *Ouranosaurus*, which was about 23 feet (7 meters) long in life, come from Early Cretaceous Period rocks in Niger, Africa. An almost complete skeleton was found in 1966 and described for science in 1976. In general, it was an animal very like *Iguanodon*, with shorter arms than legs, hooves on its fingers and toes, and a spiked thumb. However, it showed variations too. The front of the snout was flattened and beaklike, almost as in a hadrosaur, and there was a bony bulge just in front of each eye.

▲ **A robust skeleton**
Ouranosaurus was fairly typical of ornithopods except in having large neural spines. It was powerfully built, with particularly strong legs.

Why the sail?

The sail may have served as a heat-exchanger. The skin of the sail had a rich blood supply, and its large surface area worked like a radiator. As the dinosaur stood sideways-on to the sun, the sail could soak up the sun's warmth. Blood flowing from the sail then spread the heat around the body. In the early morning this process would make *Ouranosaurus* warmer and active before other sailless reptiles. So it could move fast, get to the food before the other animals, and also escape from attackers.

If *Ouranosaurus* became too hot, it could stand in the shade with the sail sideways-on to a cool breeze. Blood would carry heat from the body into the sail, and from there the heat would be blown away. Today African elephants flap their huge ears to lose excess body heat.

▲ **Stiff back, flexi-neck**
The arms and hands of *Ouranosaurus* were smaller than those of *Iguanodon*, with hooves on the second and third fingers only. The typical stiff, weight-bearing wrist joint and thumb-spike were present. The fin structure would make the backbone and tail of *Ouranosaurus* fairly rigid. However, to compensate, the cervical (neck) vertebrae and their joints show that the neck was short but ultraflexible.

Skull structure

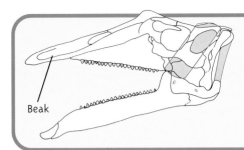

Beak

Ouranosaurus had a long, low skull with a wide snout and flat, toothless "beak," more like the bill of a duck than the snipping edge of a tortoise. The large jaws were worked by powerful muscles, which were attached to the prong at the back of the lower jaw for extra leverage. The many grinding cheek teeth resembled those of *Iguanodon*. A pair of bony bumps above the nostrils was again like the duckbilled dinosaurs rather than the iguanodontids.

Same sail

The same reasoning would apply to another sail-backed dinosaur, *Spinosaurus*. This theropod or carnivorous dinosaur lived in the same place and at the same time as *Ouranosaurus*. It was larger but it also had a back sail with spines that were even longer than those of *Ouranosaurus*, up to 6 feet (almost 2 meters). Perhaps predator and prey evolved the same answer to the same problem, each trying to gain the upper hand in the struggle for survival.

If not temperature control, then why?

Temperature regulation is one of the most convincing explanations for the sail on the back of *Ouranosaurus*. But there are other possibilities:

- The spinal extensions may have supported a fleshy hump like that of an American bison or some kinds of antelopes. The hump may have been for sexual display at courting time.
- A similar hump could be a food store of body fat, as in the camel.
- A thin sail made mainly of skin could have been brightly colored for sexual display or recognition, as in the modern lizard *Hydrosaurus* from Southeast Asia.

◄ **Prehistoric inhabitants of the Sahara**
Ouranosaurus and a gigantic crocodile, *Sarcosuchus*, lived in what was then a lush environment of rivers and forests.

DATA BASE

Name *Ouranosaurus*
Pronounced OO-ran-oh-SORE-us
Meaning "brave monitor lizard"

What it ate Plant-eater, browsing on tall ferns, cycads, and early flowering plants

Length (nose - tail-tip) 23 feet (7 meters)
Standing height 12 feet (3.7 meters)
Weight 1-2 tons (1-2 tonnes)

When it lived Middle Cretaceous Period 115 million years ago
Where it lived Africa (Niger)

Order Ornithischia (bird-hipped dinosaurs)
Suborder Ornithopoda
Family Iguanodontidae

➡ An early iguanodontid

Camptosaurus was one of the first members of the iguanodontid group known from the fossil record.

The fossils of *Camptosaurus* date mainly from the Late Jurassic and Early Cretaceous Periods 150-140 million years ago. The fact that they have been found in both Europe and western North America supports the theory of continental drift. At the time, the Atlantic Ocean was narrow, and these landmasses were probably joined to each other by land bridges.

Camptosaurus remains are especially abundant in the generally fossil-rich Morrison Formation rocks of Colorado. Skeletons of adults and juveniles have been discovered, some of the youngsters only about 4 feet (1.2 meters) in total length.

Plenty to chew on

Camptosaurus was one of the smallest and earliest iguanodontids. It may even have predated the main iguanodontid group. For its body size its skull was long, wide, and heavily built. The long snout had a large toothless beak at the front. It was designed to pull and cut off leafy vegetation on the lower branches of trees such as ginkgoes and tree ferns.

A bony plate, the hard palate, separated the mouth of *Camptosaurus* from its nasal passages above. This meant *Camptosaurus* could continue to breathe while chewing its food. Many reptiles lack this feature and must gasp for breaths as they eat. The closepacked, grinding cheek teeth also suggest that *Camptosaurus* spent plenty of time chewing (see illustration on facing page).

Primitive and advanced

In evolutionary science "primitive" does not necessarily mean old-fashioned, unsuccessful, or ultrasimple. It refers to an earlier stage in evolution. The later stages are termed "advanced." For example, sharks are "primitive" because they appeared early in the general evolution of fishes. Yet they are undoubtedly successful because they have survived for more than 300 million years and still thrive today.

Limbs and movement

Camptosaurus had several primitive features, compared with later members of the iguanodontid group. It had four hoofed toes

◀ A likely victim

Camptosaurus probably spent much time browsing on low vegetation. But many meat-eating dinosaurs lived at the same time and in the same region, such as *Allosaurus* and *Ceratosaurus*. The iguanodontid, not as large and powerful as later members of its group, could have made a filling meal. Young *Camptosaurus* may have been victims of smaller hunters, such as the agile *Ornitholestes*.

Death scene
An imaginary reconstruction of a fight to the death between *Allosaurus* (right) and *Camptosaurus* (left). *Allosaurus* was one of the largest of the big predatory dinosaurs called carnosaurs. It was similar in some ways to the great *Tyrannosaurus* but slightly smaller and, like *Camptosaurus,* lived 80 million years earlier.

on each foot, whereas *Iguanodon* itself had three. Also, the first digit or thumb had a short spur, rather than a fully fledged spike, and the second and third fingers had tips that were more like the original reptile claws rather than the hooves of *Iguanodon*.

The arms were short but sturdy, and the wristbones were joined together to form the weight-bearing structure found in later iguanodontids. With arms designed more for support than manipulation, this probably meant that *Camptosaurus* could move around on all fours. However, the legs were strong enough to support the whole body weight. So *Camptosaurus* may have spent some time walking on two feet rather than on four.

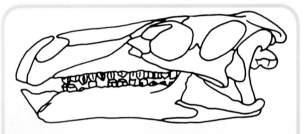

Shearing teeth
In the skull of *Camptosaurus* both cheek regions and upper jaws were hinged so that they could tilt outward. They would do this as the lower jaws rose, allowing the upper and lower sets of teeth to move past each other with a shearing-grinding motion. Later ornithopods, such as *Iguanodon*, and the hadrosaurs, such as *Edmontosaurus*, had a similar mechanism.

 **DATA BASE**

Name	*Camptosaurus*
Pronounced	Kamp-toh-SORE-us
Meaning	"flexible lizard,"

 What it ate
Plants

Length	(nose - tail-tip) 23 feet (7 meters)
Standing height	12 feet (3.6 meters)
Weight	about 1 ton (1 tonne)

When it lived	Late Jurassic to Early Cretaceous Periods 145-135 million years ago
Where it lived	U.S. (Colorado, South Dakota, Utah, Wyoming), Europe (Portugal, England)

Order	Ornithischia (bird-hipped dinosaurs)
Suborder	Ornithopoda
Family	Iguanodontidae

→ An alternative lifestyle

The dryosaurs showed features of both the *Iguanodon* and *Hypsilophodon* groups of ornithopods.

Dryosaurus was one of the largest and earliest of the hypsilophodont-type ornithopods from the Middle and Late Jurassic Period. About 13 feet (4 meters) in total length, it had a long neck, long and stiff tail, and long and slender rear legs. Its skull and teeth show that, like other ornithopods, it was a plant-eater.

Some features of *Dryosaurus* suggest it belongs in the hypsilophodont group (see pages 34-35). Others suggest it could be closely related to the iguanodontid group (see pages 22-23). A third view is that *Dryosaurus* deserves its own subgroup, ranking equally with the iguanodontids.

Among the giants

There were many other plant-eating dinosaurs in the Late Jurassic world. They include the biggest kinds of all – the massive sauropods such as *Brachiosaurus* and *Diplodocus*. They had evolved to have gigantic bulk and power, pillarlike legs, and slow, heavy movement.

Dryosaurus had evolved in a different way. The length of the leg's shin compared with its thigh (see page 21) shows that it was probably a fast runner. The bulk of its leg muscle was concentrated in the hips and thighs. These muscles were connected down to the bones in the shins and feet by long, cordlike tendons.

This design reduced the amount of

◄ **Thighbone**
The right femur (thighbone) of a small *Dryosaurus*. It comes from Tanzania, East Africa, and is 8 inches (20 cm) long.

weight near the end of the limb, which allowed the limb to be swung more rapidly and freely backward and forward with each running stride. Today's rapid sprinters, from ostriches to deer, gazelles, and horses, have the same basic energy-saving design.

A widespread dinosaur

Fossils of *Dryosaurus* have been found in a wide variety of locations, including western North America and East Africa. The remains from the Tendaguru Hills of Tanzania were originally named *Dysalotosaurus*, "lost wood lizard." But in recent years they have been closely compared with the fossils of *Dryosaurus* and found to be so similar that *Dysalotosaurus* is now generally considered to be a kind or species of *Dryosaurus*. During the Late Jurassic Period the landmasses of Europe and Africa had started to drift away from the Americas, but there may still have been land

▶ **Sniffing around**
Dryosaurus stoops down to sniff the ferns and other plants as potential food. Its slim, light build contrasts with most of the iguanodont-type dinosaurs. The toes are also longer and less designed for weight-bearing, more for gripping the ground while running.

▲ Energy-saving design
Dryosaurs, like modern deer, had strong muscles in the hips and thighs, and long shins. The design is well suited to sprinting.

bridges or an eastern route across Siberia and Alaska that linked North America to Asia.

Slim build

Dryosaurus was a generally slim animal with slender legs and only three long toes on each foot. (*Hypsilophodon* had four.) Yet there were five fingers on each hand and strong arms. The stiff tail was probably used for balance and to help turning at speed. *Dryosaurus* would have to live and feed alongside the huge sauropod herbivores such as *Apatosaurus*, *Diplodocus*, and *Brachiosaurus*. And predators such as *Coelurosaurus* and *Allosaurus* would threaten it.

Dinosaur sheep?
Unlike *Hypsilophodon*, *Dryosaurus* had no teeth at all in the front of its mouth. There was probably a toothless, horny pad at the upper front of the mouth, which closed against the horny, beaklike lower front to grasp and crop vegetation. Some modern herbivores, such as sheep and deer, have a similar toothless front to the upper jaw with which they can grasp and crop vegetation. The sharp-ridged cheek teeth at the back of *Dryosaurus*'s mouth would be used for chewing.

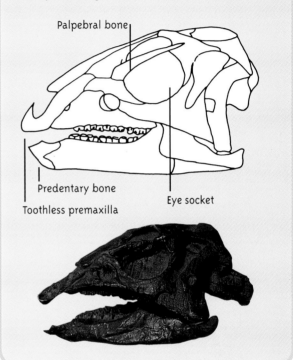

Palpebral bone

Predentary bone

Toothless premaxilla

Eye socket

DATA BASE

Name	*Dryosaurus*
Pronounced	DRY-owe-SORE-us
Meaning	"oak lizard"

What it ate
Plant-eater

Length	(nose - tail-tip) 13 feet (4 meters)
Standing height	8 feet (2.4 meters)
Weight	175 pounds (80 kilograms)

When it lived	Middle to Late Jurassic Period 160-140 million years ago
Where it lived	U.S. (Colorado, Utah, Wyoming), Africa (Tanzania), possibly also Europe (England, Romania), and Australia

Order	Ornithischia (bird-hipped dinosaurs)
Suborder	Ornithopoda
Family	Dryosauridae?

Teeth with high ridges

One of the most widespread and numerous dinosaurs of its time, *Hypsilophodon* is known from many well-preserved skeletons.

Hypsilophodon is named from its teeth, which are tall and ridged. It was one of the smallest ornithopods. The hypsilophodonts are named after it. This family, whose characteristic feature is the high-ridged teeth, includes *Othnielia* and *Tenontosaurus* (see page 34), *Orodromeus* (see page 38), and possibly *Dryosaurus* (see pages 30-31) and *Nanosaurus* (see page 34).

Up in the trees

Fossils of *Hypsilophodon* come mainly from the Isle of Wight, in southern England. They were first discovered in about 1849, and further specimens came to light in the 1850s-60s. At first they were thought to be remains of young *Iguanodon*. But in 1869-70 the eminent zoologist Thomas Henry Huxley (1825-95) realized they were from a different animal, and he renamed them *Hypsilophodon*. (Huxley also studied the links between dinosaurs and birds and many other aspects of prehistory. He strongly supported the theory of evolution by natural selection, as proposed by Charles Darwin in his 1859 book *On the Origin of Species*.)

Down from the trees

Hypsilophodon was small for an ornithopod – only waist-high to a human. Its size and other aspects revealed by those early studies

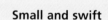

Small and swift
From the Isle of Wight fossils we can picture a small group of *Hypsilophodon* nibbling ferns, horsetails, and other low vegetation in the swamps. The size, lightness, and proportions of this dinosaur suggest it was a swift, agile runner. Its main form of defense was to dodge the attacker and dart away, using its stiffened tail for balance and steering.

suggested its similarity to the tree kangaroo of today. Many reconstructions in the first half of the 20th century showed these dinosaurs perched in trees, grasping the branches with birdlike perching feet.
In the 1970s new studies found no evidence for this tree-dwelling way of life. *Hypsilophodon* came down to earth as a fast, agile, bipedal (walking on two legs) ground-dweller.

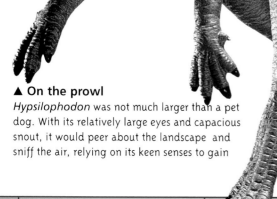

▲ On the prowl
Hypsilophodon was not much larger than a pet dog. With its relatively large eyes and capacious snout, it would peer about the landscape and sniff the air, relying on its keen senses to gain

Died together

About 23 well-preserved *Hypsilophodon* skeletons, some almost complete, have been found in

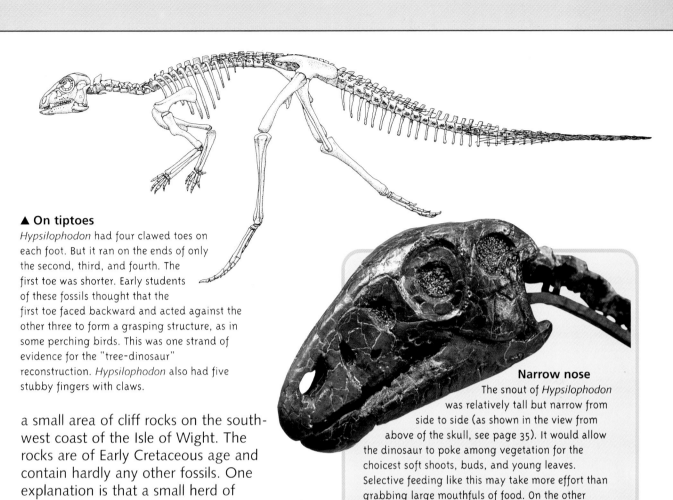

▲ On tiptoes

Hypsilophodon had four clawed toes on each foot. But it ran on the ends of only the second, third, and fourth. The first toe was shorter. Early students of these fossils thought that the first toe faced backward and acted against the other three to form a grasping structure, as in some perching birds. This was one strand of evidence for the "tree-dinosaur" reconstruction. *Hypsilophodon* also had five stubby fingers with claws.

a small area of cliff rocks on the south-west coast of the Isle of Wight. The rocks are of Early Cretaceous age and contain hardly any other fossils. One explanation is that a small herd of *Hypsilophodon* was trapped by the rising tide, perhaps in the quicksands at the edge of the shallow sea that covered much of northern Europe during this time. Further evidence for herd dwelling is discussed on pages 36-37.

Narrow nose

The snout of *Hypsilophodon* was relatively tall but narrow from side to side (as shown in the view from above of the skull, see page 35). It would allow the dinosaur to poke among vegetation for the choicest soft shoots, buds, and young leaves. Selective feeding like this may take more effort than grabbing large mouthfuls of food. On the other hand, chewing and digesting large quantities of food, of which most is unsuitable and only a little is nutritious, could use up even more energy and bodily raw material. So, *Hypsilophodon* had probably found the most efficient method of feeding.

DATA BASE

Name *Hypsilophodon*
Pronounced hip-sill-OH-foh-don
Meaning "high-ridge tooth"

What it ate
Plant-eater, probably browsing low-growing swampy vegetation such as ferns and horsetails

Length (nose - tail-tip) 7 feet 6 inches (2.3 meters)
Standing height 3 feet 3 inches (1 meter)
Weight 50 pounds (22.7 kilograms)

When it lived Early Cretaceous Period 120 million years ago
Where it lived Europe (England, Spain), possibly U.S. (South Dakota)

Order Ornithischia (bird-hipped dinosaurs)
Suborder Ornithopoda
Family Hypsilophodontidae

→ A conservative family

Hypsilophodontids were small to medium-sized ornithopods that first appeared in the Late Jurassic Period, spread across most of the world, and survived until the end of the Cretaceous Period.

The hypsilophodontids, including *Hypsilophodon* itself (see pages 32-33), probably evolved from the types of ornithopods called fabrosaurs (see pages 40-43). The hypsilophodonts evolved generally larger body size, more efficient jaws and teeth for chewing food, and big eyes for good vision. They became especially diverse during Cretaceous times in Australia.

However, the hypsilophodontids did not change very much over tens of millions of years. One of the first kinds, *Othnielia* from the Late Jurassic Period, was very similar to one of the last, *Thescelosaurus* from the Late Cretaceous Period – almost 90 million years later. Those of the species that differed most from the typical body design were the semiarmored types with two rows of bony plates, or scutes, along the back, and the largest well-known member of the group, *Tenontosaurus*.

Tenontosaurus

This very large hypsilophodontid, "sinew lizard," is known from fossils dating to the Early to Nid-Cretaceous Period at various sites in North America, including Arizona, Montana, Oklahoma, and Texas. It was up to 25 feet (7.6 meters) long and weighed around 1 ton (1 tonne). Because of its size, it is sometimes included in the iguanodontid group, but its teeth are mostly hypsilophodontid.

The arms of *Tenontosaurus* were relatively long and sturdy, so it may have spent more time walking on all fours than other hypsilophodontids. Half of its total length was the heavy, thick tail, which was stiffened by bony tendons at its end.

One famed specimen of *Tenontosaurus* was found associated with five specimens of the dinosaur *Deinonychus*. This predator, a theropod related to *Velociraptor*, had a huge claw on each foot for ripping prey. The original remains may have been washed together by chance, such as by a river in flood, before fossilizing. However, maybe something more exciting happened, such as a pack of *Deinonychus* attacking and slashing at *Tenontosaurus* (see page 49 and also volume 8 in this series).

Othnielia

This hypsilophodont lived in Late Jurassic times. Its fossils have been found in Utah and Wyoming. In 1877 a celebrated American fossil hunter and professor at Yale University, Othniel Charles Marsh (1831-99), named them *Nanosaurus* but they were renamed in his honor in 1977. Some specimens are less than 5 feet (1.5 meters) long.

Othnielia had the typical hypsilophodont build: slim body, long tail, long, slender rear limbs, and short, armlike front limbs with five-fingered hands. Its teeth were unusual because they were entirely covered in enamel, a very hard substance. Usually only the chewing

◀ **Wary feeder**
Tenontosaurus watches a flock of pterosaurs as it feeds, aware that the flying reptiles may have been disturbed by a major predator.

▶ **Early Cretaceous landscape**
A hypsilophodontid, its tail held stiffly horizontal, travels through Montana some 130 million years ago.

Other hypsilophodonts
- *Valdosaurus*, "Wealden lizard," from the Early Cretaceous Period in Europe and perhaps Africa.
- *Zephyrosaurus*, "west wind lizard," from the Early Cretaceous Period in North America.
- *Fulgurotherium*, "Lightning Ridge beast," from the Early to Middle Cretaceous Period in Australia.
- *Loncosaurus*, "Lonco lizard," from the Late Cretaceous Period in South America. However, it could be a carnivore from the very different theropod group of dinosaurs!

surfaces have such a covering. This may show that the plants it ate were very tough.

Parksosaurus
One of the last hypsilophodontids, *Parksosaurus* ("Parks's lizard") survived in Late Cretaceous times in Alberta, Canada. It was only around 8 feet (2.4 meters) long and may have perished in the great mass extinction that finished off all other dinosaurs. Like other later hypsilophodontids it had very large eyes, perhaps for searching for prey in the gloomy undergrowth.

Thescelosaurus
A widespread dinosaur of Late Cretaceous times in western North America, *Thescelosaurus*, or "wonderful lizard," was almost 12 feet (3.7 meters) long. It was a mixture of hypsilophodontid and iguanodontid features, quite bulky, with teeth at the front of its upper jaw, thighs and shins of equal length, and five toes on each foot. It was probably much slower than a typical hypsilophodont, and had rows of bony lumps or studs along its back, which gave it a type of armorplated protection.

Leaellynasaura
This hypsilophodontid is described more fully in volume 5 of this series, along with the other Early Cretaceous "polar dinosaurs" of Australia. It was a typical bipedal, parrot-beaked, plant-eating hypsilophodontid, standing only waist-high to a human. Its eyes were not just large, as in other members of the

family, but huge. So were the optic lobes, the parts of the brain that receive visual information as nerve signals from the eyes. This feature may have helped *Leaellynosaura* to survive in the seasonal cool darkness of its semipolar landscape. It also has a connection with the question whether it was cold-blooded or warm-blooded (see volume 5).

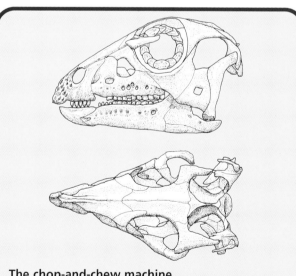

The chop-and-chew machine
At the front of its mouth *Hypsilophodon* had incisor-type teeth in the middle bone of the upper jaw. They probably bit down onto a horny beak that covered the bone of the lower jaw. This part of the mouth chopped vegetation. The cheek teeth were tall and sharp-ridged, almost like chisels. During chewing, the lower jaw moved up within the upper jaw, making the upper bones tilt outward and the lower ones tilt inward. The cheek teeth ground past each other, slicing and chewing food, while the cheek pouches kept it in the mouth. As the teeth wore out, they were replaced regularly.

Herd of dinosaurs?

Did dinosaurs live in groups, even interacting socially with each other? If so, why? Hardly any reptiles today are herd-dwellers...

It is one of the basic laws of nature that herbivores fall prey to carnivores. So herbivores need protection from carnivores. It comes in various forms, such as large body size and strength, sharp weapons like tusks or hooves or horns or antlers, sharp senses and extreme speed for quick escape, or tough plates or shields of armorplating on the body.

Another aspect of defense is "safety in numbers." There are various advantages to group living for herbivores, as follows.

1 Always on guard
Most animals in a group are feeding or resting at any one time. But the chances are that there are a few members who are alert and on guard, looking and listening and sniffing for potential danger. If it is detected, they can warn the others, by sights and sounds, and trigger a mass escape.

2 Confusion in the ranks
In a fleeing herd of zebra, a flock of birds, or a shoal of fish it is difficult to pick out an individual. The patterns and sounds they make change constantly as the members dodge, turn, and wheel at speed, like one huge "superorganism." So it is hard for a predator to track and attack a single member.

3 Finding food
Locating food is another advantage. This is especially noticeable as a flock of birds pecks its way across a meadow. The birds not only look for food but also watch each other. When one finds a rich source, it stops and eats. The others notice and gather around to see if there is enough to share. Likewise, in city centers pigeons or gulls soon gather around the tourist who has brought the bread or a bag of seeds.

4 Swamping the predator
Another advantage of group-dwelling comes during the breeding season. If all herd members produce babies at about the same time, there is suddenly a huge number of offspring. Animals are very vulnerable during this early period of life. But a limited number of predators can take only a limited number of young. The large number of possible victims swamps the hunters.

5 Collective defense
A predator might find it quite easy to overcome a single animal. But overcoming several of them — especially parents protecting their offspring — is a much more daunting prospect. So predators therefore generally do not attack herds of animals. They watch and wait around the edges until a young, old, or sick member gets separated from the herd or left behind.

▲ **Purposeful flight**
For birds such as these black-headed gulls the main advantage of flocking together is finding food and nesting sites.

▲ **Safety in numbers**
Perhaps the herbivore dinosaurs lived together in herds for protection like these blue wildebeest in Africa.

▲ **Many feet**
Collections of fossilized footprints, like this *Iguanodon* specimen,

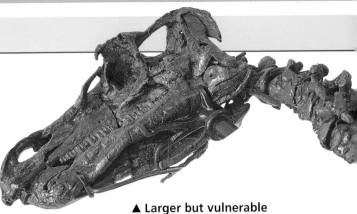

▲ Larger but vulnerable
Iguanodon was not very well protected. Living in groups may have made up for its lack of body defenses.

Evidence for ornithopod group living

There is evidence that some dinosaurs, including certain ornithopods, may have formed groups. Of course, some animals of the same kind gather together today for a reason — a rich source of food or a safe place to shelter or hibernate. But there is little social interaction, and when the reason for coming together has gone, they soon go their separate ways. Did some ornithopods form herds in which the members interacted socially and traveled, fed, and bred together?

• (Lack of) body defenses

Most of the ornithopods, especially the earlier types, were relatively small and defenseless creatures. *Hypsilophodon* was speedy and agile, but if cornered, it was hardly big and strong enough to put up much of a fight. Even *Iguanodon* had a medium bulk and two thumb-spikes, but not much more. A large, well-equipped predator could easily overcome one individual. The lack of body defenses may suggest that living in groups would protect the animals from danger.

• Footprints

Fossilized footprints of dinosaurs have been found all over the world. In 1997 sections of tracks were discovered in Australia that could link into a trail some 50 miles (80 kilometers) long. From a print's size and shape it is usually possible to say which main kind of dinosaur made them.

Trackways from southern England show that many *Iguanodon*-type dinosaurs passed the same way. The prints seem to be from a variety of individuals, and all face in much the same direction. It is more likely that a herd on the move made them, rather than one or a few individuals repeating the same journey over days, weeks, or months. This is partly because the environmental conditions that are needed for footprints to be preserved are very specialized and don't usually last much time. A typical *Iguanodon* footprint is about 2 feet (60 cm) across, with the three large digits showing clearly, and the foot is "pigeon-toed," that is, it points slightly inward.

• Fossil accumulations

At some sites many dinosaur skeletons are discovered together. It is rarely possible to say if they actually died together. The bones could have been piled up over a long period, for example, by floodwaters at a bend in a river. It is this kind of chance that makes the legendary "elephants' graveyards" of modern times.

More than 30 *Iguanodon* specimens were found in a Belgian mine (see page 12). Perhaps they slid or fell into a ravine. Or they may have fallen in a mad stampede or suffered a landslide. On the other hand, floods may have washed the carcasses or bones into the gorge, even over several years.

The 20-plus *Hypsilophodon* specimens from the Isle of Wight (see pages 32-33) are in the same state of preservation, which suggests that the animals were rapidly buried in mud. Even their body postures are similar. So it looks as though they did both live and die together. Possibly they were all overcome by the same flood, fell into the same quicksand, or were cut off by the same rising tide.

▲ A circle of protection
Fully grown African elephants are awesome creatures, but their young need the protection offered by family and herd living.

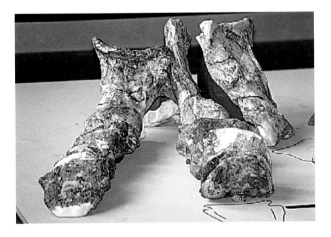

◀ Printmakers
Iguanodontid footbones made footprints that can be easily recognized. In many places they have been found in great numbers making up long trackways.

Nests, eggs, and babies ▶

Nests, eggs, and babies

In the 1980s amazing discoveries in Montana caused a revolution in our ideas about the way dinosaurs produced their young.

In 1978 a chance find in a rock-and-fossil store in Bynum, Montana, led to the discovery of the preserved bones of dinosaur babies. Further digging at rocky hills near the town produced the fossilized remains of hundreds of dinosaur eggs, the nests they were laid in, the babies that had hatched from them, and in some cases eggs containing babies that had not yet hatched. The hills were investigated from 1979, and one has become known as "Egg Mountain."

The eggs, nests, and babies included two kinds of ornithopods that lived and bred at the same time and in the same region. One was the hadrosaur *Maiasaura* (see volume 9 in this series). The other was a hypsilophodont, *Orodromeus*.

Neat nests

Orodromeus was very similar to *Hypsilophodon*, though slightly smaller. Dozens of *Orodromeus* nests were discovered, regularly spaced about 6 feet (2 meters) apart. This was a dinosaur breeding colony, probably on an island in what was once a shallow Late Cretaceous lake. "Egg Mountain" could have been "Egg Island."

Each nest was a shallow bowl-shaped area of scraped sand containing a number of eggs. In one of the best-preserved examples there are 19 eggs. They are laid in a neat pattern, spiraling out from the nest's center. The eggs were probably covered with vegetation and more sand to keep them hidden and warm.

Hatched and gone

The empty eggshells in the nests of the much larger hadrosaur *Maiasaura* were broken and fragmented. Probably they were trampled on by the youngsters that stayed in the nest after hatching.

The empty shells of *Orodromeus* were in better condition. In some the lower half of the shell lay almost undisturbed in the fossilized sand. It seems that the youngsters broke their way out through the upper half and left the nest right away.

Inside the eggs

There are many jumbled bones of *Orodromeus* hatchlings at the site. There are also some whole eggs. A CAT scanner (used in medical clinics to look at human tissue) made images of the interiors. The bones of the embryos, or unhatched babies, were visible on the scans. So the fossil eggs were cut open,

Herd of dinosaurs?

and the fossil embryos within carefully studied – the first time this had been done for any dinosaur.

Caring crocodile

Traditionally, reptiles have not been considered caring parents. But in the 1970s observations of crocodiles showed that the mother stays near the area of riverbank where she buried her eggs. When the babies are ready to hatch, she hears them squeaking and helps them emerge. She then carries them to the water in the safety of her mouth and even guards them for a time. We are still finding exciting new information, not only about dinosaurs but also about living reptiles. There is still a lot to learn.

◀ **Rapid exit**

This model of the nest, eggs, and babies of *Orodromeus* shows the hatchlings breaking out of the eggs. Scientists think that the babies left the nest immediately to fend for themselves, so they did not need parental care.

▶ **Caring parents**

Emperor penguins are caring parents. The father looks after the egg until the baby hatches.

Parental care

The legbones and joints of the unhatched babies were well developed. They would have been strong enough to allow the youngsters to leave the nest right after hatching. That would account for the untrampled eggshells.

In contrast, the legbones and joints of unhatched *Maiasaura* babies were not well developed. This meant the youngsters would have had to stay in the nest, hence the trampled shells. Researchers have gone on to propose that the *Maiasaura* babies must have been fed by caring dinosaur parents!

Fossilized eggs and other evidence of a small predatory dinosaur, *Troodon*, complete the picture. It was probably a meat-eater that followed the herbivore herds, bred on the fringes of their colonies, and snatched their eggs and babies to feed itself and perhaps its own offspring.

DATA BASE

Name *Orodromeus*
Pronounced OR-roe-droe-MEE-us
Meaning "mountain runner"

What it ate
Plant-eater, probably browsing on low-growing vegetation

Length (nose - tail-tip) 6 feet 6 inches (2 meters)
Standing height 3 feet (1 meter)
Weight 40 pounds (18 kilograms)

When it lived Late Cretaceous Period 70 million years ago
Where it lived U.S. (Montana)

Order Ornithischia (bird-hipped dinosaurs)
Suborder Ornithopoda
Family Hypsilophodontidae

Dinosaur with two names? ▶

Dinosaur with two names?

A small, early ornithopod dinosaur may have been given two names, *Fabrosaurus* and *Lesothosaurus*. Or it may not.

The fabrosaurs, along with the heterodontosaurs (see pages 46-47), were some of the earliest members of the ornithopod group. They first appeared at the end of the Triassic Period and persisted until the beginning of the Cretaceous Period, although individual types apparently survived for relatively short times.

Trashcan dinosaurs?

Fabrosaurs were small, slim, lightweight, agile, bipedal plant-eaters. At least, they probably were. Apart from a couple of the better-known members, their fossils are scattered and fragmentary. It may be that fabrosaurs are a "trashcan" group into which various small, ornithopod-type dinosaurs have been dumped for convenience. This sort of thing has happened in other areas of paleontology, including the grouping and naming of our own human ancestors.

As more remains are found, the fabrosaurs could lose their status as a group. The members could be split into several new groups or assigned to other, already existing groups.

First discovery of the group

The first fabrosaur discovery was made in the Purbeck area of Dorset, southern England, by Samuel Beckles, who hunted for fossils in his spare time. The fossils included small, slender jaws with deep-rooted, leaf-shaped teeth that had slightly spiky edges. The animal was named *Echinodon* ("spiny tooth") by Richard Owen (see page 17). He believed it was a lizard, but it was then transferred to the dinosaur group. It may be a fabrosaur. Or it may be a heterodontosaur. It could even be a cousin of the armored dinosaur *Scelidosaurus*.

A southern reptile

In 1964 a small piece of broken fossil jaw, with teeth similar to those of *Echinodon*, was found in southern Africa. The rocks that contained the fossil were from the very Late Triassic or Early Jurassic Period. That made them about 50 million years older than

African fabrosaur

The femur, or thighbone, of a fabrosaur. The pen next to it gives a size comparison

▶ **Adaptable eater**

Lesothosaurus (or *Fabrosaurus*) was only about 3 feet (1 meter) long and probably an adaptable feeder. It could snip off plant material with its horny front "beak" and also grab small prey such as insects, amphibians, and little lizards. The flexible neck would probe to find the newest, softest shoots and buds, since the teeth could not cope with tough leaves.

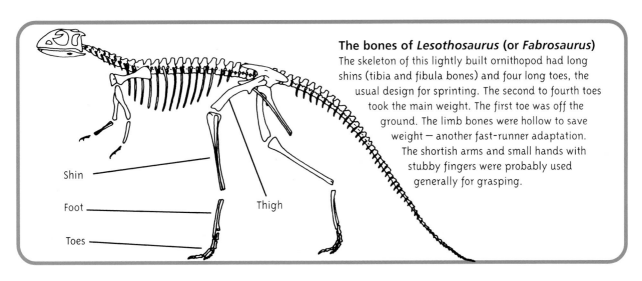

The bones of *Lesothosaurus* (or *Fabrosaurus*)
The skeleton of this lightly built ornithopod had long shins (tibia and fibula bones) and four long toes, the usual design for sprinting. The second to fourth toes took the main weight. The first toe was off the ground. The limb bones were hollow to save weight — another fast-runner adaptation. The shortish arms and small hands with stubby fingers were probably used generally for grasping.

Shin

Foot

Toes

Thigh

those containing the *Echinodon* remains, which were dated from the very Late Jurassic or early Cretaceous Period. Although the two sets of fossils were similar, they came from different times and places, so the new find was called *Fabrosaurus australis* ("Fabre's southern lizard").

A similar find
In the 1970s a full-scale fossil expedition in southern Africa turned up yet another set of similar remains. They included part of a skeleton and so were a much bigger find than the *Fabrosaurus* fossils. They were found in the same area and from rocks of a similar age – Late Triassic-Early Jurassic. The

location was the "Red Beds" near Mafeteng, in the small country of Lesotho.

At first this new find was thought to be another specimen of *Fabrosaurus*. But then, because the *Fabrosaurus* evidence was so skimpy, it was thought unscientific to try to make detailed comparisons between the two or to treat them as examples of the same animal. Until further studies or fresh finds were made, it was safer to give the newer find a different name. In 1978, therefore, its name was changed to *Lesothosaurus*, after the region.

Back again to the first name
More recently, some scientists have again begun to think that *Lesothosaurus* really was the same as *Fabrosaurus*. If so, all the remains should be grouped under the first scientific name given (this is traditional practice). So *Lesothosaurus* will now be renamed *Fabrosaurus*, unless further studies or fresh finds show that the two animals were different.

More about fabrosaurs ▶

More about fabrosaurs

It is possible that some fabrosaurs were summer sleepers, awakening when rains ended the drought.

A small herbivore

Lesothosaurus (or *Fabrosaurus*) was a very small dinosaur, hardly larger than a big pet cat. It was slender and flexible, with a small head, long neck, slim body, and lengthy tail. To make up for its smallness and lack of obvious bodily defenses, it had sharp senses that could detect danger early, and a fast, darting getaway.

Sleeping during drought?

Fossils indicate that the general landscape in southern Africa during Late Triassic-Early Jurassic times was dry, with scrubby semidesert. The layers of stone in the Red Rocks could suggest alternating wet and dry seasons. If so, *Lesothosaurus* (or *Fabrosaurus*) may have nipped off leaves and tender new shoots from low-growing plants during moist times. Then it may have gone into a deep sleep for the drought.

Hiding away for a long sleep during a dry season is well known in the animal world. Many creatures of desert regions do it, from snails and insects to frogs, lizards, and bats. This hot-season sleep is known as estivation (a cold-season sleep is called hibernation).

Other fabrosaurs

In addition to the relatively better-known *Lesothosaurus/Fabrosaurus*, several other creatures that may belong to the fabrosaur group have been proposed. But the evidence is mostly based on a few fossil fragments, and each type may well belong to another group.

- *Echinodon* from the Late Jurassic Period of England (as mentioned). It was only 2 feet (about 60 cm) long, with small, sharp teeth and probably some bony armorplating. However, it was more likely to have been a member of the armored dinosaur group, the scelidosaurs.
- *Nanosaurus* ("dwarf lizard"), some 3 feet (90 cm) long. Fragmentary remains were found in Late Jurassic rocks in Colorado. It could have been a relative of *Hypsilophodon* (see pages 32-33).
- *Alocodon* ("wing tooth") and *Trimucrodon* ("three-pointed tooth"), both known only from bits of teeth found in Jurassic rocks in Portugal.
- *Gongbusaurus* ("Gongbu lizard") from Jurassic times in China. It was about 5 feet (1.5 meters) long. Like *Nanosaurus*, it may have been a cousin of *Hypsilophodon*.

New teeth for old

What is the evidence that *Lesothosaurus* (or *Fabrosaurus*) estivated during the driest times?

DATA BASE

Name	*Lesothosaurus* (or *Fabrosaurus*)
Pronounced	Le-SOO-too-sore-us (or FAB-row-sore-us)
Meaning	"Lesotho lizard" (or "Fabre's lizard")

What it ate Plant-eater, probably browsing on tender parts of low, scrubby desert vegetation

Length	(nose - tail-tip) 3 feet 3 inches (1 meter)
Standing height	30 inches (75 centimeters)
Weight	about 7 pounds (3 kilograms)

When it lived	Late Triassic to Early Jurassic Periods 210-200 million years ago
Where it lived	Lesotho in southern Africa, possibly Venezuela in South America

Order	Ornithischia (bird-hipped dinosaurs)
Suborder	Ornithopoda ?
Family	Fabrosauridae ?

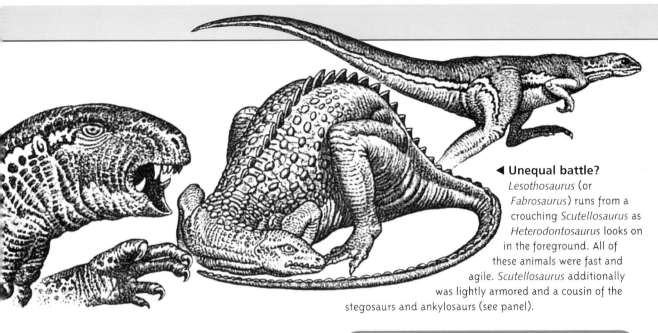

◄ **Unequal battle?**
Lesothosaurus (or *Fabrosaurus*) runs from a crouching *Scutellosaurus* as *Heterodontosaurus* looks on in the foreground. All of these animals were fast and agile. *Scutellosaurus* additionally was lightly armored and a cousin of the stegosaurs and ankylosaurs (see panel).

Two fossil specimens were preserved curled together, and their jaws contained full sets of sharp, unused teeth. Normally, reptile teeth are replaced continuously as they wear away. The bodies of *Lesothosaurus* (or *Fabrosaurus*) were preserved, along with heavily worn teeth, which may have dropped out of their jaws. Could it be that while these animals went to sleep for the dry season, new teeth grew and pushed out the old?

▼ **A successful recipe**
Lesothosaurus may be a bit of a mystery, but it certainly combined speed with agility. This picture shows it racing across the dry, rocky Late Triassic landscape.

Armorplated fabrosaur?
Scutellosaurus was once placed in the fabrosaur group. It was an armored type of dinosaur, with bony plates (or scutes) in its skin, like those of a crocodile. Its fossils were discovered in Arizona. The armorplating was not as thick, heavy, or extensive as in some of the later armored dinosaurs such as the ankylosaurs. It was more of a compromise between protection and speed, being thick enough to offer some shieldlike defense but not so heavy as to slow the creature to a crawl. The extremely long tail helped balance the heavy body when the animal was running on two back legs. However, the front legs were long compared with those of other fabrosaurs, so *Scutellosaurus* may have walked on all fours too.

Many experts now regard *Scutellosaurus* not as a fabrosaur but as a close relative of *Scelidosaurus*. So it is described in more detail in volume 10 of this series, which deals with stegosaurs, ankylosaurs, and similar plated and armored dinosaurs.

→ Different teeth, different tasks

Heterodontosaurus was yet another small, lightweight, agile, bipedal type of ornithopod. But instead of the usual reptile teeth, it had varied teeth in its jaws.

The heterodontosaurs were very similar in size and shape to the fabrosaurs shown on the previous pages. They were little, light, lithe, plant-eating ornithopod dinosaurs, moving mainly on the two larger rear limbs.

The heterodontosaur group is known mainly from fossils dating back to the Late Triassic and Early Jurassic Periods found in southern Africa and North America. One of the earliest finds, in 1911, was a piece of jawbone with teeth still embedded in it. The owner was named *Geranosaurus*. A second discovery was called *Lycorhinus angustidens*, "wolf snout with sharp teeth." It had long, spearlike, canine teeth in the front of the upper and lower jaws, with well-worn cheek teeth behind them.

Unreptilian teeth

From its teeth *Lycorhinus* was first thought to belong to the mammallike reptiles. These reptiles evolved differently from the dinosaurs. The mammallike reptiles thrived during the Later Permian and Early Triassic periods – before the Age of Dinosaurs had really begun. Mammallike reptiles are thought to have been the ancestors of the first true mammals, which appeared toward the end of the Triassic Period perhaps 220 million years ago.

A variety of teeth

The main reason for this proposal was the different types of teeth fossilized in the mouth of *Lycorhinus*. Most mammals have teeth of different shapes in the same mouth, which are suited to different tasks (see page 46). The mammallike reptiles have this feature too. But further finds, especially *Heterodontosaurus* itself – the name means "different-toothed lizard" – confirmed that these small creatures really were dinosaurs from the ornithopod group.

Three types of teeth

Heterodontosaurus had three types of teeth. The small, sharp, almost spiky teeth in the front of the upper jaw bit against the standard ornithopod horny beak at the front of the lower jaw. They were for snipping and cropping. Behind them was a pair

◄ Strong-armed dinosaur

Heterodontosaurus was a lightly built, agile creature capable of rapid running. But its forearms were larger and stronger than in other members of the group. The long fingers had well-developed claws, and the hand was mounted on a flexible wrist. Such sturdy arms and hands may have been good for digging up and handling plant food, and also for moving on all fours.

of extraordinary fang- or tusklike teeth in both upper and lower jaws. They looked like the large canine teeth of today's dogs. As the mouth closed, the lower set fitted into socketlike grooves in the opposing jaw. And behind each of these tusks was a row of 12 cheek teeth, used for grinding and pulping food. (See the skull drawing on page 46.)

No other dinosaur, indeed, hardly any reptile group has teeth that are so different. *Heterodontosaurus* probably had fleshy skin flaps that formed cheeks too. This arrangement would allow it to gather food and chew efficiently, and so perhaps survive on a greater range of plants than a dinosaur with teeth that were all much the same.

Why tusks?

Meat-eating animals such as cats and dogs have long, pointed canine teeth for stabbing their prey and tearing the flesh. But *Heterodontosaurus* was almost certainly a herbivore. So why did it have tusklike teeth?

- A clue may come from fossil evidence for its environment, which was dry and scrubby semidesert. Perhaps the tusks were for digging up succulent plant parts from the dry soil. (Warthogs today grub with their tusks.) *Heterodontosaurus* also had fairly powerful arms and large, strong hands, which may have been used for digging too.

Jaw structure
The cheek teeth of *Heterodontosaurus* formed two long grinding surfaces for mashing plant food. The lower jaw had the normal hinge joints with the skull, allowing up-and-down movement only. The lower jawbones had joints that allowed them to tilt inward as they passed up inside the upper-jaw teeth. (In later ornithopods the bones of the upper jaw and skull were hinged, with the result that they bowed out over the lower jaw.)
The fossil teeth show much wear, suggesting that *Heterodontosaurus* tackled very tough, abrasive plant food.

- Another suggestion is that the tusks were for defense. Again, modern vegetarian animals such as wild pigs have them, and are not afraid to slash at enemies and inflict terrible wounds.
- A third proposal is that the tusks may have been a sign of sexual or social status. In elephants, hippos, and walruses, bigger tusks mean a mature, powerful male who has a greater chance of mating with females. A similar fossil skull found in the same rock formations, and named *Abricotosaurus*, lacks the tusks. It may have been a specimen of *Heterodontosaurus* of the other sex, probably the female.

Knee-high dinosaur
Heterodontosaurus was named in 1962, and several well-preserved skulls and skeletal remains have now been uncovered. In life its head would have been about knee-high to a human. The overall size and proportions of the bones are a lot like those of the fabrosaurs and indicate a fast runner. However, the legs were built more heavily and some of the bones were fused together for strength.

Hand

Foot

→ More varied teeth

Many of the known heterodontosaurs come from southern Africa or South America.

A fine set
The "yawning" snow leopard conveniently displays all its different kinds of teeth, including the small front incisors, the large pointed canines, and the ridged molars, or cheek teeth.

Mammal teeth

Most mammals have teeth of different shapes, which are suited to different tasks. They include:

- chisellike incisors at the front for gnawing and cutting;
- longer and more pointed, spear-shaped canines, or "eye teeth," for stabbing and ripping;
- broader, flatter-topped teeth in the cheek region, called premolars and molars, for crushing and grinding.

We can see these types of teeth in our own mouths, although the differences are seen more clearly in the mouth of a cat or dog.

Pisanosaurus

One of the first ornithopods, and even one of the first ornithischian dinosaurs, was possibly *Pisanosaurus* ("Pisano's lizard"). It lived during the Late Triassic Period in South America. But the fossilized remains of the pelvis or hipbone,

which is the main bone used to work out whether an animal belongs to ornithischians or saurischians (see page 9), are fragmentary. So the exact identity and relationships of *Pisanosaurus* are disputed.

Pisanosaurus had low, triangular-crowned teeth for grinding food. Ornithopods and similar ornithischians had teeth like this, arranged in the same way. *Pisanosaurus* probably also had fleshy cheek pouches,

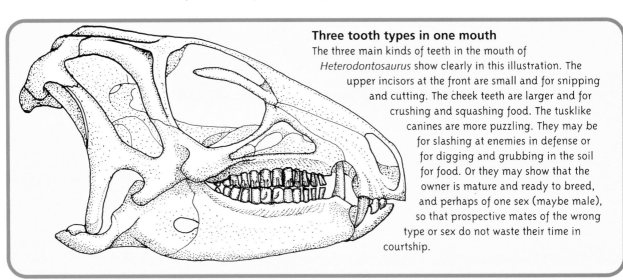

Three tooth types in one mouth
The three main kinds of teeth in the mouth of *Heterodontosaurus* show clearly in this illustration. The upper incisors at the front are small and for snipping and cutting. The cheek teeth are larger and for crushing and squashing food. The tusklike canines are more puzzling. They may be for slashing at enemies in defense or for digging and grubbing in the soil for food. Or they may show that the owner is mature and ready to breed, and perhaps of one sex (maybe male), so that prospective mates of the wrong type or sex do not waste their time in courtship.

Tusks for tasks
The warthog has large tusks, long, sharp teeth that protrude from the mouth.

another ornithopod feature.

If *Pisanosaurus* was a heterodontosaur, its presence in South America could be evidence that this landmass was linked at the time to the stronghold of the heterodontosaurs, Africa.

Other heterodontosaurs

These members of the heterodontosaur group are known from less complete remains, and their identification may change.

- *Geranosaurus* ("crane lizard") was similar to *Heterodontosaurus*. Its remains date from Early Jurassic times and were found in South Africa.
- *Lycorhinus* ("wolf snout," see page 44) was another tusked heterodontosaur, like *Heterodontosaurus* itself. It was another Early Jurassic, South African member of the group.
- *Abricotosaurus* ("wide-awake lizard") is known from a well-preserved skull that is like the skull of *Heterodontosaurus* but without the tusks. Was it a female

Heterodontosaurus (see page 45)? It lived in Late Triassic-Early Jurassic times in southern Africa.
- *Lanasaurus* ("wooly lizard") was yet another heterodontosaur from early Jurassic South Africa.

DATA BASE

Name	*Heterodontosaurus*
Pronounced	HETT-er-owe-DONT-owe-sore-us
Meaning	"different-toothed lizard"

Length	(nose - tail-tip) 3 feet (90 centimeters)
Standing height	2 feet (60 centimeters)
Weight	7 pounds (3 kilograms)

What it ate
Plant-eater, probably browsing on low-growing vegetation, snipping off the leaves and chewing them thoroughly before swallowing

When it lived	Early Jurassic Period 200 million years ago
Where it lived	Africa (South Africa, Lesotho)

Order	Ornithischia (bird-hipped dinosaurs)
Suborder	Ornithopoda
Family	Heterodontosauridae

What happened to the ornithopods?

Various groups of ornithopods came and went during most of the Age of Dinosaurs. But even these adaptable plant-eaters disappeared during the mass extinction that wiped out all dinosaurs.

The ornithopods were generally widespread and numerous, as far as we can tell from the fossil record. They thrived especially through the Jurassic and Cretaceous Periods.

- The early and small types, the fabrosaurs and heterodontosaurs, were moderately successful in the early part of the Jurassic Period. They lived alongside the massive sauropod dinosaurs from the saurischian group, nibbling low-growing vegetation.
- Toward the end of the Jurassic Period the hypsilophodonts, with their more efficient chewing jaws and teeth, began to flourish. By the middle of the Cretaceous Period they were diverse (for ornithopods) and had spread almost all around the world. A few types, such as *Thescelosaurus* and *Parksosaurus*, both from North America, lasted until the Late Cretaceous Period (see page 35).
- The iguanodontids, with their cheek teeth specialized for crushing and grinding, were another very successful group of ornithopods. They lived across the world throughout the middle of the Cretaceous Period.

▲ On the move
A herd of iguanodontids negotiates its way around the massive fallen trunks of conifer trees and other huge plants in the Early Cretaceous Period.

- In the second half of the Cretaceous Period the iguanodontids seem to have been replaced by a related group of ornithopods and possibly their descendants the hadrosaurs. The last iguanodontids, such as *Mochlodon* (see page 23), survived until the end of the period in areas where the hadrosaurs did not take over.
- The hadrosaurs (see volume 9 in this series) were expanding and diversifying right until the end of the Age of Dinosaurs.

The mass extinction

However, the ornithopods could not survive the huge catastrophe that brought the Age of Dinosaurs to a relatively sudden end 65 million years ago. The mass extinction wiped out not only all the dinosaurs but also the swimming reptiles such as plesiosaurs and ichthyosaurs, the flying reptiles called pterosaurs, various other kinds of animals, and certain types of plants too.

What killed the dinosaurs?

Suggested causes of the mass extinction at the end of the Cretaceous Period include:

- a huge meteorite crashing into the earth, throwing up clouds of dust that blotted out the sun and brought sudden global cooling. Lack of warmth and light killed many plants, affecting the food chains, and lowered temperatures affected cold-blooded animals too;
- a massive series of volcanic eruptions covering the planet with smoke, ash, and choking poisonous fumes;
- rapid climate changes around the world, linked to the drifting of the continents around the globe, changing wind patterns, and altered sea currents;
- epidemics of disease that affected only selected groups of living things;
- competition from increasingly successful mammals and birds, which perhaps ate the eggs and young of much bigger creatures;
- genetic "staleness," when the same group of living things has been evolving for a very long time and runs out of genetic variation to cope with changing conditions;
- large amounts of dangerous rays, heat, and light from outer space, such as solar explosions on the sun, storms of meteorites or comets, or even a vast passing mist of

▼▲ At their mercy
Ornithopod dinosaurs, being plant-eaters (above), would always be at ther mercy of hunting dinosaurs such as the dromaeosaur or "raptor" *Deinonychus*. During the Early-Middle Cretaceous Period a pack of these dromaeosaurs could tackle the large hypsilophodontid *Tenontosaurus* (below left, see also page 34). Or an individual could track down and leap on a smaller single prey such as *Hypsilophodon* itself (bottom).

dust known as a giant molecular cloud (GMC).

These causes and possible combinations of them are discussed in detail in volume 12 of this series.

The future of dinosaurs

The ornithopods and other dinosaurs are long gone. But we continue to dig up their fossils, reconstruct their skeletons and bodies, discover better ways of studying them, and make better guesses about how they lived, fed, bred, and died. A new find may show that the fabrosaurs are really a "trashcan" group, or that *Iguanodon* made nests for its eggs, or that the back sail of *Ouranosaurus* was for social signaling rather than temperature control. These continuing discoveries make dinosaurs some of the most fascinating and mysterious creatures ever to walk the earth.

Index

PICTURE CREDITS
The publishers gratefully acknowledge the following for the use of illustrations.
T top
B bottom
C centre
R right
L left

Ardea 6, 16L, 17TL
W. T. Blows 31CR
S. and S. Czerkas: *Dinosaurs: A Global View* (London, Dragon's World, 1991) 8, 22
Digital Vision 21TL, 36CR, 37BR, 39TL, 47
Douglas Henderson 27CL, 35T, 43B, 48, 49TR
Institut Royal des Sciences National de Belgique 10, 11TL, 11BR, 12T, 17CR, 37TR
Natural History Museum Photo Library 9C, 14 (4 images), 15T, 16TR, 19 (3 images), 21BR, 30CL, 32CR, 33CR, 38, 45TR

Planet Earth Pictures 29T
Salamander Picture Library 12BR, 13T, 15B, 18T, 18B, 20, 24B, 25TL, 25CR, 26CR, 26BL, 27TL, 28, 29CR, 30B, 31TR, 32BL, 33T, 34, 35BR (2 images), 40-41, 41T, 43T, 44, 45B (3 images), 46BL, 49BL (2 images)
Sandown Museum, Isle of Wight 23, 36BR, 37BL
Science Photo Library 9TL, 17CL
John Sibbick 24CR
South African Museum of Natural History 40BL
Superstock 7, 31TL 36TR, 39CR, 46TR

The publishers have endeavoured to observe the legal requirements with regard to the rights of suppliers of photographic and illustrative material.

Glossary

Note These are explanations of terms as they relate to dinosaurs and other prehistoric animals. Some of the terms have more general biological, geological, or scientific meanings.

Advanced Appearing later in a sequence or more recently in time; one of the later of its kind.

Age of the Dinosaurs The time when dinosaurs were the dominant large animals on land. Usually taken to mean most of the Mesozoic Era, from the Middle-Late Triassic Period 230-220 million years ago to the end of the Cretaceous Period 65 million years ago.

Ankylosaur An armored dinosaur with lumps, plates, or slabs of protective bone in its skin, and a large bony lump on the end of the tail for use as a club.

Archosaurs ("ruling reptiles") A reptile group that included dinosaurs, pterosaurs, and also the crocodiles of today.

Articulated In a skeleton, having bones still in position next to each other, as they were when the animal was alive, rather than jumbled up or scattered.

Bipedal Walking or moving about on two legs, usually the back pair (like ourselves).

Carnivore An animal that eats mainly the meat or flesh of other creatures.

Carnosaur A general name for any medium-sized or large predatory or meat-eating dinosaur that ran on its two larger back legs, like *Allosaurus* or *Tyrannosaurus*. Not a true classification group.

Carpal Bone in the wrist.

Caudal To do with the tail. A caudal vertebra is a backbone in the tail.

Ceratopsian A horned and/or frilled dinosaur, with horns on the face or head and a large rufflike neck frill, such as *Triceratops*.

Cervical To do with the neck.

Clavicle The collarbone or similar bone in the upper chest and shoulder region.

Coelurosaur ("hollow-tailed lizard") A general name for a small, slim, and lightweight dinosaur such as *Coelophysis* from early in the Age of the Dinosaurs. Not a true classification group.

Cold-blooded (more accurately, "ectothermic") Referring to an animal that does not generate heat inside its body and whose body temperature therefore varies with the temperature of its surroundings.

Continental drift The slow movement over millions of years of the major landmasses about the surface of the earth. The earthís crust is made up of sections called lithospheric plates, which float about on the layer of molten rock underneath, carrying the continents with them. The process is called plate tectonics.

Convergent evolution The evolution of two or more different types of animals in such a way that they come to look or be similar because they occupy the same habitat or face the same problems. Two examples are the wings of bats and pterosaurs, which look similar on the outside but have different bone patterns, and the overall streamlined body shape of marlin (living fish), ichthyosaur (extinct reptile), and dolphin (mammal) for moving fast through the sea.

Cranium The topmost curved dome of the skull, mainly above the face and around the brain ñ the ìbrain case.î

Cretaceous One of the periods or timespans of the earthís history, lasting from about 144 to 65 million years ago; the last period of the Mesozoic Era and the Age of the Dinosaurs.

Digit Finger or toe.

Digitigrade Walking and running on the toes or even the toe-tips (digits).

Disarticulated In a skeleton, having bones jumbled up or scattered about, not in position next to each other, as they were when the animal was alive.

Dromaeosaur A small to medium-sized active, predatory dinosaur that walked on its back legs, with sharp teeth and claws, such as *Deinonychus*. Some dromaeosaurs are called raptors.

Ectothermic Of an animal, unable to generate heat inside its body. Its body temperature therefore varies with the temperature of its surroundings.

Endothermic Of an animal, able to generate heat inside its body. Its body temperature stays constant and usually high, despite the varying temperature of its surroundings. Today only mammals and birds are endothermic.

Evolution The slow process of change in living things, usually gradual and taking thousands or millions of years.

Extinction The dying out of every member of a group of living things, with the result that the species or group has gone forever.

Femur Thigh or upper legbone.

Fenestra A gap, hole, or ìwindow,î usually in a bone.

Fibula Bone in the lower leg, sometimes called the calfbone.

Gastric To do with the stomach or general belly region. Gastroliths are "stomach stones" swallowed by dinosaurs on purpose to help grind up food in the gizzard, stomach, and other digestive parts.

Geology The scientific study of the earth, its formation and history, its rocks and other materials, and the processes and events that shape them.

Hadrosaur A duckbilled dinosaur, an ornithopod-type dinosaur with a mouth shaped like a duckís beak.

Herbivore An animal that eats mainly plants, including leaves, fruit, stems, shoots, buds, roots, and so on.

Heterodontosaur A small, plant-eating dinosaur with teeth of different shapes, some long and sharp like tusks or fangs and others flatter for crushing food. A member of the larger ornithopod group.

Humerus Bone in the upper arm.

Hypsilophodont A small, slim, agile plant-eating dinosaur with front upper teeth in a beaklike mouth, plus rear upper and lower chewing teeth. A member of the larger ornithopod group.

Jurassic One of the periods or timespans of the earthís history, lasting from about 208 to 144 million years ago; the middle period of the Mesozoic Era and the Age of the Dinosaurs.

Keratin A body substance (protein) that forms our fingernails and toenails, also our hair and mammal fur, hooves, and horns, and also the feathers of birds and scales of reptiles.

Lumbar To do with the lower back.

Mandible Lower jawbone.

Matrix The rock around a fossil, encasing or containing it.

Maxilla Bone forming part or all of the upper jaw.

Metabolism A general name for the many chemical processes that go on inside a living thing.

Metacarpal Bone in the palm part of the hand.

Metatarsal Bone in the sole part of the foot.

Natural selection The way that the natural struggle for survival allows some individuals to live and breed and in so doing to pass their genes (coded information contained in the cells) to the next generation. Stronger and fitter individuals are înaturally selectedî to survive, weaker ones are not.

Nodosaur An armored dinosaur with lumps (nodules), plates, slabs, and spines of protective bone in its skin, but lacking a large bony lump on the end of the tail.

Occipital At the rear of the skull, usually low down near the neck.

Omnivore An animal that eats meat, plants, and any other food.

Orbit The hole or socket in the skull for the eye.

Ornithischian ("bird-hipped") A dinosaur with hipbones similar in general structure to those of a bird. There were several major groups of ornithischian dinosaurs, which were all plant-eaters, including the ornithopods, ceratopsians, stegosaurs, ankylosaurs, and pachycephalosaurs.

Ornithomimosaur An ostrich dinosaur, a small to medium-sized slim, lightweight dinosaur with long, powerful back legs, long neck and beaklike mouth, like *Struthiomimus*. It had the general shape and proportions of an ostrich.

Ornithopod ("bird foot") A large group of dinosaurs with birdlike feet, including *Iguanodon* and the hadrosaurs.

Pachycephalosaur A thick-headed, bone-headed, or helmet-headed dinosaur such as *Pachycephalosaurus* with a thickened layer of bone on the top of the skull, presumably for butting and battering.

Paleontology The scientific study of extinct life forms, especially as revealed by their fossils.

Pectoral To do with the shoulder region.

Pelvic To do with the hip region.

Pelvis Hipbone, made of individual bones joined or fused together.

Permian One of the periods or timespans of the earth's history, lasting from about 290 to 248 million years ago; the last period of the Paleozoic Era and the period before the Age of the Dinosaurs.

Phalanges Bones in the digits (fingers and toes).

Plantigrade Walking and running flat on the soles of the feet.

Predator An animal that hunts and kills other creatures – known as its prey – for food.

Prey An animal that is hunted and killed by another, the predator.

Primitive Appearing early in a sequence or long ago; one of the first of its kind.

Prosauropod A medium-sized to large dinosaur such as *Plateosaurus* showing development of the sauropod features of small head, long neck, barrellike body, stout, pillar-shaped legs, and a long, tapering tail.

Pterosaurs A extinct group of flying reptiles that lived throughout the Age of the Dinosaurs.

Quadrupedal Walking or moving about on four legs.

Radius Bone in the lower arm or forearm.

Raptor Variously interpreted as "thief," "predator," or "plunderer." Usually refers to the small to medium-sized active, predatory dinosaurs that walked on their back legs, with sharp teeth and claws, especially dromaeosaurs such as *Velociraptor*.

Saurischian ("lizard-hipped") A dinosaur with hipbones similar in general structure to those of a lizard. There were two major groups of saurischian dinosaurs – all of the meat-eating theropods and all of the large to giant-sized plant-eating prosauropods and sauropods.

Sauropod A large to giant-sized dinosaur with a small head, long neck, barrellike body, stout, pillar-shaped legs and a long, tapering tail, such as *Diplodocus*.

Scapula Shoulder blade bone.

Scute A bony or horny structure in the skin, such as a flat, shieldlike plate.

Sedimentary rock Rock formed from compacted, cemented particles or sediments, usually laid down in horizontal layers on the bottoms of seas, lakes, and rivers.

Sediments Pieces or particles of rock such as gravel, sand, or silt, worn off or washed away by weathering and erosion and eventually deposited on the ground.

Stegosaur A plated dinosaur, a large, four-legged plant-eater with plates or spikes of bone probably standing upright along its neck, back, and tail, as in *Stegosaurus*.

Sternum The breastbone or similar bone at the front of the chest.

Taphonomy The scientific study of collections, gatherings, and accumulations of objects, and how, when, where, and why they occur.

Tarsal Bone in the ankle.

Tertiary One of the periods or timespans of the earthís history, lasting from about 65 to 2 million years ago; the first period of the Cenozoic Era and the period after the Age of the Dinosaurs.

Theropod ("beast-foot") A general group of dinosaurs that mostly walked on their two back legs and included all the meat-eaters, from tiny *Compsognathus* through the small and medium-sized dromaeosaurs to the large carnosaurs.

Thoracic To do with the chest.

Tibia Bone in the lower leg, sometimes called the shinbone.

Torpor Deep sleep or long period of inactivity, for example during very cold weather.

Trace fossils A fossil that did not come from a body part but that reveals the activity or presence of a living thing, such as a footprint or nest.

Triassic One of the periods or timespans of the earth's history, lasting from about 248 to 208 million years ago; the first period of the Mesozoic Era and the Age of the Dinosaurs.

Ulna Bone in the lower arm or forearm.

Vertebra A backbone or spinal bone, one of the chain of bones making up the spinal column.

Warm-blooded (more accurately, "endothermic") Referring to an animal that generates heat inside its body and whose body therefore stays at the same, usually high temperature, despite the varying temperature of its surroundings. Today only mammals and birds are endothermic.

Published by
Grolier Educational, Sherman Turnpike, Danbury, Connecticut 06816

Library of Congress Catalogue-in-publication Data
Age of the Dinosaurs

Volume 1 Origins of the Dinosaurs
Volume 2 The Early Dinosaurs
Volume 3 The Carnosaurs
Volume 4 The Sauropods
Volume 5 Dinosaurs and Birds
Volume 6 Dinosaur Cousins
Volume 7 The Ornithopods
Volume 8 Dinosaur Pack-hunters
Volume 9 The Hadrosaurs
Volume 10 Armored Dinosaurs
Volume 11 The Ceratopsians
Volume 12 The Last of the Dinosaurs

Set title: The Age of the Dinosaurs
ISBN 0-7172-9413-7

Volume 7:
ISBN 0-7172-9407-2

Project Editor and Manager Ingrid Cranfield

Design Manager John Strange

Designer Megra Mitchell
(Mitchell Strange Design)

Printed and bound in Singapore

A word of caution
This book, like others about dinosaurs, shows realistic-looking animals and describes them with great confidence. But no human has even seen a real living dinosaur. Our knowledge about them comes mainly from fossils . Using fossils to work out what a dinosaur looked like and how it lived involves guesswork – very intelligent, well-informed, and scientifically based, but still guesswork. The fossil evidence can be interpreted in various ways, and new fossils regularly change our ideas. This is why the study of dinosaurs is filled with lively debate and heated discussion and is so fascinating!